History, Politics and
Policy-making in Education

The Bedford Way Papers Series

A full list of Bedford Way Papers, including earlier books in the series, may be found at www.ioe.ac.uk/publications.

History, Politics and Policy-making in Education

*A festschrift presented
to Richard Aldrich*

Edited by
David Crook and Gary McCulloch

Bedford Way Papers

First published in 2007 by the Institute of Education, University of London,
20 Bedford Way, London WC1H 0AL
www.ioe.ac.uk/publications

© Institute of Education, University of London 2007

British Library Cataloguing in Publication Data:
A catalogue record for this publication is available from the British Library

ISBN 978 0 85473 786 4

Front cover: Richard Aldrich, Public Orator in 2007
  (photo by Success Photography).
Back cover, top: photo by Stearn & Sons.

Typeset by Keystroke, 28 High Street, Tettenhall, Wolverhampton
Printed by DSI Colourworks

Contents

List of contributors

Vincent Carpentier is Lecturer in History of Education at the Institute of Education, University of London.

Michèle Cohen is Professor of Humanities and Social Sciences at Richmond American International University in London.

David Crook is Senior Lecturer in History of Education at the Institute of Education, University of London.

Dennis Dean formerly taught at the Institute of Education, University of London.

Peter Gordon is Emeritus Professor of History of Education at the Institute of Education, University of London.

Roy Lowe, OBE is a Visiting Professor at the Institute of Education, University of London.

Gary McCulloch is Brian Simon Professor of History of Education and Dean of Research and Consultancy at the Institute of Education, University of London.

Roger Openshaw is Professor of History of Education at Massey University, New Zealand.

Wendy Robinson is Professor of Education at the University of Exeter.

Janet Soler is Senior Lecturer in Education at the Open University.

Ruth Watts is Professor of Education at the University of Birmingham.

Geoff Whitty is Director of the Institute of Education, University of London.

Foreword
Geoff Whitty

Richard Aldrich has had a long and happy association with the Institute of Education since he arrived in Bloomsbury in September 1973. He was immediately recognised as an outstanding lecturer, tutor and supervisor, and he has made a vital contribution to the development and growth of teaching and research in the history of education at the Institute.

Richard's early publications focused on the interaction of politics and education in the nineteenth century. His research then broadened significantly and he became a leading national and international authority on the history of education, contributing numerous high-quality articles, chapters and books to the field. The introductory chapter by the editors sets out his many academic achievements. It is hard to single out a particular text within such an accomplished body of work, but his style is well demonstrated in such books as *An Introduction to the History of Education* (1982) and his collection of writings *Lessons from History of Education* (2006), as well as his co-authored work with Peter Gordon and Dennis Dean, *Education and Policy in England in the Twentieth Century* (1991).

His writings have had considerable impact on contemporary scholarship, as can be seen in the work represented in this book. Vincent Carpentier's chapter on the economic and historical aspects of policy-making in education is an interesting example of this: it highlights the strength of an alliance between two different disciplinary areas, an approach which Richard has always encouraged. Similarly, Michèle Cohen's chapter on the role of the mother in eighteenth-century educational discourse emphasises the contribution of the family to education, another key theme of Richard's work. Other chapters similarly complement and continue his interests.

Beyond his teaching and research, Richard's academic leadership and administration at the Institute has been influential and always principled, for example during his time as Head of the Department of History, Humanities and Philosophy and then the History and Philosophy Group. He became a professor in 1995 and, although he was due to retire in 2002, we were delighted that, as the author of the Institute's history, he remained in post for our centenary year. In 2003 Richard assumed the title of Emeritus Professor of History of Education, but at a time when others might anticipate a slowing down in the pace of life he has continued to write and to contribute significantly to the Institute's work. For example, he continues to serve as the Institute's very distinguished Public Orator.

Richard's engagement with his research field is profound and extensive, and his writing is always insightful. I am delighted that he should be the subject of this very timely festschrift.

Acknowledgements

We should like to express our appreciation to each of the authors who have contributed to this festschrift, and also to the following international colleagues, who offered strong encouragement and support: Anja Heikkinen, Katsutoshi Namimoto, Tom O'Donoghue, Bill Reese and Clive Whitehead.

The Director of the Institute of Education, Geoff Whitty, enthusiastically supported the idea of an edited collection in honour of Richard Aldrich and we are grateful to him for supplying the Foreword. Thanks are also due to Averil Aldrich (who was in on the secret before Richard), James Baldock, Cathy Bird, Marianne Coleman, Belinda Dearbergh, Helen Green, Brigid Hamilton-Jones, Marleen Laurman, Sandy Leaton-Gray, Elaine Peck, Sally Sigmund and Deborah Spring.

We hope that the book will be a lasting tribute to Richard and that he will enjoy reading the contributions that follow.

David Crook
Gary McCulloch

Introduction

David Crook and Gary McCulloch

> My delight in history was acquired as a young lad and has remained to
> this day. My belief that there are lessons to be drawn from history, and
> not least from history of education, has developed over many years as
> a student and teacher of the subject.
>
> (Aldrich 2006a: 1)

At the time of writing this introduction, plans were in hand for
Professor Richard Aldrich to celebrate his seventieth birthday on 10
June 2007 in the presence of his family, close friends and colleagues
at The Valley, Charlton, his home from home, or rather one of two
homes from home. Richard's intellectual home, since 1973, has been
the Institute of Education, University of London, and those of us who
work in its History of Education section shall be forever grateful for
the inheritance he has left us. Richard's past achievements, and his continuing guidance since his formal retirement in 2003, remain enduring
influences upon our teaching and research.

This is not the first scholarly collection dedicated to Richard. Three
years ago, Clive Whitehead and Tom O'Donoghue, from the University
of Western Australia, edited a collection of essays by friends and
colleagues working in universities beyond these shores. It is our hope
that this festschrift, edited and predominantly authored by historians
based in the UK, and featuring several chapters by Institute colleagues,
will be viewed as an essential complement to that special issue of

1

Education Research and Perspectives (Whitehead and O'Donoghue 2004).

A Charlton boy, born in 1937, the Sunday and nursery schooling of Richard Edward Aldrich was experienced as an evacuee in Talgarth, Brecon, Wales. Following his return to South London, he successfully sat the eleven-plus examination one year early, at Deansfield Junior School, Eltham, and proceeded in 1947 to the Roan School for Boys, Greenwich. It was here that a history teacher, Kenneth Binnie, inspired the 'young lad' to apply to read the subject at Fitzwilliam House, Cambridge, in 1955. Over the next three years, like many who had gone before him, and many who came after, Richard's key influence was Fitzwilliam's Director of Studies, Leslie Wayper, an army educationist and historian. Wayper's death, in 2006, was marked by an obituary in *The Times* which noted that 'Generations of Fitzwilliam historians look back on his teaching and his friendly encouragement with affection' (*The Times*, 28 April 2006, obituary: 72).

Upon graduation with an upper second, Richard commenced a secondary history Postgraduate Certificate in Education (PGCE) course at King's College, University of London, in 1958. His tutor at King's was A.C.F. ('Rudolph') Beales, subsequently holder of the Chair in History of Education, a 'superb lecturer', whose Friday performances in the Beveridge Hall of Senate House were the highlight of a distinguished line-up of University of London educationists, including the philosopher of education Louis Arnaud Reid and P.E. Vernon, the psychologist, both from the Institute of Education. Beales's lectures, Richard remembers, had 'structure and jokes', and provided a model that was to make its mark on his own lecturing style. The sometime observation of Dennis Dean, a contemporary at Cambridge and later a close Institute colleague, that 'You are the inheritor of Beales' is remembered as a huge compliment (editors' interview with Richard Aldrich, 11 September 2006).

After completing the PGCE, Richard commenced a teaching post at Godalming County School, where he stayed for six formative years, becoming a more confident and 'developed person'. 'Teaching did more for me than I did for the pupils', he remembers with characteristic modesty (ibid.). Thereafter, he secured a first higher education post at Southlands College of Education, a Methodist college for the education and training of teachers in Wimbledon. As a lecturer and then senior lecturer in history at Southlands, Richard taught and supervised on a variety of programmes, including the PGCE and the increasingly important Bachelor of Education (BEd) degree. His time at the college, between 1965 and 1973, saw him shoulder increasing administrative responsibilities, but he also successfully completed his MPhil thesis, under Beales's supervision, entitled 'Education and the political parties, 1830–70' (1970). He then proceeded to register for a doctorate in educational history, again under Beales, focusing on the career of Sir John Pakington, the leading nineteenth-century Conservative parliamentary champion of national education.

The opportunity to establish and run a BEd teaching option in History of Education at Southlands brought Richard into closer contact with the emerging community of British historians of education. The History of Education Society (HES) had been founded in December 1967, with David Bradshaw of the Sheffield City College of Education as chairman. Beales had not initially been an enthusiast for the society, but his successor at King's was Professor Kenneth Charlton from Birmingham University, a founding HES committee member. A doctoral student of Charlton from 1972, Richard began, from this point, to play an active part in HES conferences and remembers from the outset being struck by the friendly welcome accorded him by Professor Brian Simon, whose remarkable scholarship over a generation significantly advanced the field (see Aldrich 1994).

From the time of J.W. Adamson's appointment as professor, in 1903, it was King's College, rather than the Institute of Education, that had been the University of London's principal centre for history of education. King's was also highly respected at a national level, at a time when other universities could boast such leading historians as Harry Armytage (Sheffield), Peter Gosden (Leeds) and Brian Simon (Leicester). A 1942 proposal by the Institute's director, Fred Clarke, that it should establish a chair in history of education had not come to pass (Aldrich 2002: 123), but a first lecturing post was eventually advertised in 1973. The work of the Institute's History Department, led by Professor Hedley Burston, had burgeoned and staff whose principal expertise lay in the area of history *in* education had found themselves having to teach more history *of* education. Having developed his profile in both areas at Southlands, Richard applied for the post, though he thought it likely that it would be offered to someone who already held a doctorate. To his surprise, he was appointed. It was later intimated that his association with King's had been more beneficial than he had assumed, when applying to a University of London 'rival'. He was seen as well placed to keep alive the King's traditions of excellence within the Institute.

Richard's arrival at the Institute in 1973 coincided with that of a new director, William Taylor, who, at the first Academic Board meeting of the year, seemed strangely familiar. They had, in fact, encountered each other some 20 years earlier, when the latter had completed a teaching practice at the Roan School.

Based in a less-than-satisfactory former hostel, number 36 Bedford Way, on a site now occupied by the Royal National Hotel, facing the Institute's current building, which was nearing completion, Richard joined a relatively large History Department, led by Burston. Three of Burston's former PGCE students, Alaric Dickinson, Peter Lee and Don Thompson, were developing a significant profile in the area of history teaching in schools and were relieved to hand over to Richard their history of education responsibilities. Burston himself could claim an expertise both in history *in* and history *of* education, but his interests in the latter related principally to the contribution of James Mill (e.g. Burston 1973). During his first ten years at the Institute, the PGCE and supervision of teaching practice, involving a great deal of cross-London travel, was a major part of Richard's work, and also that of Dennis Dean and Margaret ('Peggy') Bryant (until her retirement in 1981). Peggy's friendship and support made her another key influence: Richard wrote a warm tribute in 2006, following her death at the age of 90 (Aldrich 2006c). The PGCE, in those days, offered some opportunities for students to pursue small research projects relating to the history of education, but formal teaching of this specialism was limited to a diploma course, offered in conjunction with King's in the less-than-popular slot of Friday evenings.

From 1973 a succession of articles, based on Richard's MPhil, were published in the *British Journal of Educational Studies*, the *Journal of Educational Administration and History* and the *History of Education Society Bulletin*. By setting aside half a day each week for research, in surroundings that became more comfortable after the opening of the Bedford Way building in 1976, Richard completed his PhD and more publications followed, beginning with a monograph about Pakington (Aldrich 1979). Involvement in committee work played a part in helping Richard to feel 'more of an Institute of Education person and less of a King's person' (editors' interview with Richard Aldrich, 11 September 2006), and in 1979 he launched an Institute Master's course in History of Education, though care was taken not to overlap with the teaching of Kenneth Charlton and Evelyn Cowie at King's. The course recruited very strongly in its early years: teachers, head teachers and local authority inspectors frequently gained financial backing to complete the course as part-timers, while full-time students were more typically those taking sabbaticals or coming from overseas. Recognition from the Economic and Social Research Council (ESRC) gave the MA course a status, and the associated studentships secured some high-calibre applicants. One former ESRC scholarship holder, Wendy Robinson, now a professor of education, is a contributor to this collection (Chapter 9).

By the early 1980s, Richard was a leading national figure in the field of history of education. He joined the HES committee and soon began a five-year stint as secretary. Later, between 1989 and 1993, he served as president of the HES and played a pivotal role in defending the field in a difficult climate which saw it removed from teacher training courses and adversely affected by changes in educational research funding. His ideas and publications profile developed significantly from the 1980s. *An Introduction to the History of Education* (1982) filled an important gap in the market for MA students, and collaborations with Dennis Dean and Peter Gordon (the latter being Chair of the History and Humanities Department from 1989 to 1991) produced a further course textbook (Gordon *et al.* 1991) and two indispensable biographical dictionaries (Aldrich and Gordon 1989; Gordon and Aldrich 1997). Both Dean and Gordon have contributed to this collection (Chapters 6 and 5, respectively).

The 1980s and 1990s saw Richard build up a strong base of research students from the UK and overseas. Additionally, established and early career historians of education from around the world came to Bedford Way to spend their sabbaticals, complete publications or conduct research in the Institute's archives, excited by the possibility of working with Richard. In the first chapter Michèle Cohen recalls Richard's support during a period she spent as a visiting fellow. Vincent Carpentier, another contributor (Chapter 2), first came to the Institute as a doctoral student in the mid-1990s and later secured a European Commission Marie Curie Fellowship, with Richard as his supervisor.

Richard managed to amass responsibilities far faster than he secured promotions. At another university, in the UK or overseas, he might have become a professor sooner than 1995, when he secured a personal chair at the Institute. But staying put had nevertheless presented him with opportunities. Invitations to teach and lecture overseas, for example in Australia, Brazil, Canada, Japan and the United States, as well as in many parts of Europe, galvanized his reputation as a leading international scholar. He was to serve a three-year term as chair – then president, after spearheading a major reform of its structures, publications and finances – of the International Standing Conference for the History of Education (ISCHE) from 1994. Ruth Watts, who followed Richard's path from the presidency of the HES to the executive of ISCHE, pays tribute in this festschrift to his work in both organisations (Chapter 4). Not only did he lead the field in the UK, he was also its principal international diplomat.

The relationship between educational history, politics and policy-making has been a central feature of Richard's work since he first registered for an MPhil with Rudolph Beales more than 40 years ago. His writings have emphasised the role of individuals and interest groups in their broader social and cultural contexts, often adding an extra dimension overlooked by scholars who have pursued narrower analyses focusing on social class or gender. He has brought out the continuities of education over time, as well as the changes, as demonstrated, for example, in his comparison between the subjects of the 1988 National Curriculum and the 1904 *Secondary Code* (Aldrich and White 1998).

His earliest and perhaps his abiding fascination lay (or lies) in the nineteenth century – Richard ranks his biography of Joseph Payne (1995), founder of the College of Preceptors and the first professor of education in Britain, alongside the Institute history (2002) as his proudest academic achievements – but his scholarship has also encompassed the twentieth and twenty-first centuries. The imperatives of political presentism have demanded the application of historical perspectives, and Richard has frequently found himself supplying the context for the latest White Paper or Education Act for the press, radio or television. Under the banner of *historical perspectives* he has contributed a wide range of articles and chapters, on subjects ranging from apprenticeship to educational standards, and from mathematics to teacher training. No subject or time period has been off the Aldrich radar (see Aldrich 2000), the tensions and complementarities between public and private education providing a further recent example of such work (Aldrich 2004).

A useful working definition of history, which Richard has regularly used, quoted here from his inaugural professorial lecture, is that 'it is about human activity with particular reference to the whole dimension of time – past, present and future' (Aldrich 1997: 3). His leadership of a HES study group, of Master's course modules and his own writings have demonstrated some clear benefits of applying historical perspectives to current educational issues, though some dangers of inexpertly applying such perspectives have also been identified (ibid.: 7–12).

In what might be regarded as his own most political piece of writing, Richard, together with Patricia Leighton, an education lawyer, argued in the mid-1980s that the Butler Act had run its course, and asked whether it was *Time for a New Act?* (1985). This view was not well received in all quarters, with some critics associating the argument with initiatives being pursued by the Conservative Right. Politically, what happened next went far beyond what had been proposed in the monograph, so it cannot be regarded as the blueprint for the 1988 Education Reform Act. Nevertheless, this 'Bedford Way Paper' stands as testimony to the possibilities for historical analysis to explain and influence contemporary educational policy.

In 1993 the then Conservative secretary of state asked a question that caused Richard to write to *The Times*. The letter merits quotation in full:

> Sir, 'Why don't people feel they own state education as they feel they own the health service?' was the question posed by the Education Secretary, John Patten, in Valerie Grove's interview ('State education can be saved. Discuss', January 22), as he waved before her the latest 'fat, grey education bill, "the longest in history with 255 clauses".'
>
> Could it be because the major theme in recent educational legislation has been a massive increase in control and ownership by the politicians of central government?
>
> Yours faithfully, RICHARD ALDRICH, University of London, Institute of Education, Department of History, Humanities and Philosophy, 20 Bedford Way, WC1. January 22.
>
> *(The Times*, 2 February 1993: 17)

The counter-question posed here by Richard was placed at the heart of a successful bid for research funding to the Leverhulme Trust, leading in turn to *Education for the Nation* (1996). Another research project, this time funded by the Nuffield Foundation, focused more intently on the process of central government departmental cultures and policy-making. This also produced a major publication (Aldrich *et al.* 2000).

Each of the chapters presented in this volume links to the overall organising theme of *History, Politics and Policy-making in Education*. In the first chapter, focusing on the ambiguous figure of the mother in eighteenth-century educational discourses, Michèle Cohen notes associations between strong political government and the critical role of the mother. This is followed in Chapter 2 by a reasoned appeal, by Vincent Carpentier, for economists and historians to work in concert better to understand and inform educational policy-making. Chapter 3 is a biographical study, by David Crook, of Sir Ernest Graham-Little. For more than 40 years, Graham-Little was heavily involved in university, as well as Westminster, politics. Chapter 4 by Ruth Watts returns to the politics of gender, focusing on the contributions made by early twentieth-century women associated with the educational work of Birmingham City Council, while Peter Gordon in Chapter 5 examines the role of Her Majesty's Inspectorate in shaping, and on occasions resisting, the direction of Board of Education policy between 1918 and 1945.

Dennis Dean's micro-political study of the period 1965–8 (Chapter 6) addresses some highly sensitive issues and difficulties encountered by a Labour government seeking to harmonise its policies on race relations, immigration and education. By contrast, in Chapter 7 Roy Lowe, Richard's contemporary, whose career as a historian of education has run in close parallel, paints on a wider canvas, applying historical perspectives to answer the key question of 'Who decides what children learn and how they should learn it?' Roger Openshaw, the only overseas-based contributor to this volume, is the author of Chapter 8, co-written with Janet Soler, which addresses the political influences that shaped national policies towards reading and literacy, concentrating on the years between 1968 and the election of Margaret Thatcher as British prime minister in 1979. The penultimate chapter (9) sees Wendy Robinson identify an 'English model' for understanding the education of gifted children. She argues that certain historical understandings of giftedness engendered ideological and political resistance which, even now, is sometimes still evident. Finally, Gary

McCulloch, who succeeded Richard as professor upon his retirement from the Institute, in Chapter 10 analyses possible associations between educational history and national security, a topic frequently presented as the most troubling political issue of our age.

There is so much more to say about Richard Aldrich that cannot be explored in depth here. For example, he has actively participated in almost every HES conference for the last 30 years, including a number in the late 1980s and early 1990s when the feeling among some – though never Richard – was that 'the end is nigh'. At the 2004 conference he became an honorary life member of the HES. Other significant achievements have included the following: chairing the monthly history of education seminars, instituted by Beales, at the University of London's Institute of Historical Research (see Aldrich 2006b); being appointed as an associate editor for the revised *Oxford Dictionary of National Biography* published in 2004; serving as a director of the General Teaching Council Company and Trust and as an editorial board member for many learned journals based in the UK and overseas.

His own scholarship has been recognised by the awards of fellowships from the Royal Historical Society and the Royal Society of Arts, and a collection of Richard's writings was recently published in Routledge's prestigious *World Library of Educationalists* series (Aldrich 2006a), the equivalent, for education professors, of being inducted into the Rock and Roll Hall of Fame. His approaches to historical methodology remain fresh, but also rigorous. A recent article reinforced the historian of education's three duties: to the people of the past; to our own generation; and to search after the truth (Aldrich 2003).

At the Institute of Education, since 1973, Richard has loyally served five directors, regularly proving capable of providing solutions to the knottiest problems. He has sat on almost all of its major committees and, since 1993, has been the Institute's Public Orator. In this latter capacity, thousands can testify to his gift for balancing the solemn and proud traditions of the academy with a joyous sense of fun.

The contributors to this volume join us, the editors (and also countless numbers of students) in wishing Richard good health and happiness, to be enjoyed with Averil, their children and grandchildren, long beyond his current landmark birthday. We sincerely thank him for his national and international academic leadership, support and friendship.

References

Aldrich, R. (1979) *Sir John Pakington and National Education*. Leeds: University of Leeds.

— (1994) 'The real Simon pure: Brian Simon's four-volume history of education in England'. *History of Education Quarterly*, 34(1), 73–80.

— (1995) *School and Society in Victorian Britain: Joseph Payne and the new world of education*. New York: Garland.

— (1996) *Education for the Nation*. London: Cassell.

— (1997) *The End of History and the Beginning of Education*. London: Institute of Education.

— (2000) 'A contested and changing terrain: history of education in the twenty-first century'. In D. Crook and R. Aldrich (eds) *History of Education for the Twenty-first Century*. London: Institute of Education.

— (2002) *The Institute of Education 1902–2002. A centenary history*. London: Institute of Education.

— (2003) 'The three duties of the historian of education'. *History of Education*, 32(2), 133–43.

— (ed.) (2004) *Public or Private Education? Lessons from history*. London: Woburn Press.

— (2006a) *Lessons from History of Education: The selected works of Richard Aldrich*. London: Routledge.

— (2006b) 'The Institute of Historical Research, University of London'. *History of Education Researcher*, 77, May, 11–14.

— (2006c) 'Margaret (Peggy) Bryant 1916–2006'. *History of Education Researcher*, 78, November, 59–60.

Aldrich, R. and Gordon, P. (1989) *Dictionary of British Educationists*. London: Woburn Press.

Aldrich, R. and Leighton, P. (1985) *Education: Time for a new act?* London: Institute of Education.

Aldrich, R. and White, J. (1998) *The National Curriculum Beyond 2000: The QCA and the aims of education.* London: Institute of Education.

Aldrich, R., Crook, D. and Watson, D. (2000) *Education and Employment: The DfEE and its place in history.* London: Institute of Education.

Burston, W.H. (1973) *James Mill on Philosophy and Education.* London: Athlone Press.

Gordon, P. and Aldrich, R. (1997) *Biographical Dictionary of North American and European Educationists.* London: Woburn Press.

Gordon, P., Aldrich, R. and Dean, D. (1991) *Education and Policy In England in the Twentieth Century.* London: Woburn Press.

Whitehead, C. and O'Donoghue, T. (eds) (2004) 'Essays in honour of Professor Emeritus Richard Edward Aldrich'. *Education Research and Perspectives,* 31(2), special issue.

1 Mothers of sons, mothers of daughters: the ambiguous figure of the mother in eighteenth-century educational discourse

Michèle Cohen

The ideas presented in this chapter were first researched during a term I spent working with Richard Aldrich as a visiting fellow in the Department of History and Philosophy at the Institute of Education, University of London. I am grateful to Richard for his warm encouragement at the time, and his continuing generosity and interest in my work, his rigorous scholarship and his exacting standards of historical thought.

'Mothers, especially bad ones, loom large in many early eighteenth-century texts, yet they continue to remain invisible in most studies of Augustan culture', wrote Toni Bowers in *The Politics of Motherhood* (1996). What Bowers calls the 'virtual silence of critical discussion' (1996: 3) of early modern motherhood is reflected in the absence of index entries for 'mother' or 'motherhood' in early social histories of the family, such as Lawrence Stone's *The Family, Sex and Marriage 1500–1800* (1977) and Randolph Trumbach's *The Rise of the Egalitarian Family* (1978).[1] There is, however, one domain in which mothers have long been visible: as their children's early educators. This role of mothers, well established before our period, was seen to be their 'Principal Care' in the early eighteenth century, and was 'senti-mentalised' by mid-century as in this poem by Thomas Marriott:

> The Females, the first Rudiments of Speech,
> The brightest Orators, and Poets teach;
> The wisest, greatest, of what-e'er Degree,
> Were first instructed, on a Mother's Knee. . .
> (Bowers 1996: 158)

The role of mothers as educators of their young children has played an important part in the development of women's education, for women themselves argued that they could not be expected to fulfil that function unless they were educated. The early eighteenth-century call on women to learn grammar is one instance of this concern. In *A Grammar of the English Tongue*, Gildon and Brightland encouraged women to learn the grammar of English not only to express their thoughts clearly and correctly, but because they were among the 'most numerous Teachers of it' (1967 [1711]: Preface). Thomas Wilson, Bishop of Sodor and Man, even claimed that the improvement of the nation depended on mothers' knowledge of grammatical English: teaching their children to speak correctly would help them towards their 'Good Fortune'; and since women's 'Voice, Ear and Tongue' were more elegant than men's, it was their moral duty to learn grammar. Women had to harness their 'natural talents to good purpose', like the mother of the Gracchi, who 'contributed very much to the forming of the eloquence of her sons' (1729: 38). John Locke took it for granted that mothers would teach their children to read, and he even encouraged them to teach their sons Latin 'if she will but spend two or three hours in a day with him, and make him read the Evangelists in Latin to her' (1922 [1693]: §177, 145–6). This role was also potentially empowering, as educationist John Burton explained to an audience of young ladies in the 1790s. Because the domestic arena privileges women as early instructors of their children of both sexes, and children are the 'future hopes of the Community', from the most private of all spaces, women, he argued, have direct influence on the most public of all spaces, the polity: 'political Government may be said to derive from the strength of the nursery' (1793: II, 87, 92, 95). Women thus ensured the health of the nation. It was Mary Wollstonecraft who expanded the idea into a powerful 'feminist' argument for women's education. 'As the care of children in their infancy is one of the grand duties annexed to the female character by nature, this duty would afford many forcible arguments for strengthening the female understanding. . . . To be a good mother a woman must have sense, and . . . independence of mind' (1995 [1792]: 243). This she can only achieve by being allowed to govern her own conduct. The role of the mother as educator has been treated as a relatively straightforward one in the historiography. As Michael McKeon notes in *The Secret History of Domesticity*, 'the most important locus of the housewife's governance was, by consensus, her responsibility for the early education of children' (2005: 184–5).

In this chapter, however, I want to complicate this conventional representation by looking at an aspect of the role of the mother as educator which has generally been overlooked. Parallel to the cosy image of the sentimental and responsible mother is another, a sort of anti-mother, the mother who displays a sort of 'excessive motherhood'. She is the 'overfond' mother. The concept of the overfond mother, argues Bowers, originated with Allestree, who 'coined the truism that mothers can fail either by loving their children too much, or by loving them too little'. For Bowers, the overfond mother is, therefore, just one of several manifestations of failed motherhood, which she explains by reference to the theme of 'mother-blame' in our culture. Bowers simplifies precisely what I want to complicate. I want to suggest that the overfond mother occurs not merely as an instance of 'mother-blame' but within a specific discourse, which provides a powerful frame for its appearance, development and persistence: the education and character formation of males in families of rank and wealth in the eighteenth century.

In *The Spectator* (364), Steele tells the story of a widowed Lady, whose dying husband has entrusted her with the management of their

16-year-old son, of whom she is extremely fond. The boy, whom Steele describes as having 'middling parts', has just distinguished himself in front of the Vicar and an assembly of the neighbourhood ladies. His mother is convinced that he is such a great scholar that he is now beyond 'Book-Learning' and ready to go on the grand tour, to France and Italy, to learn about 'Men and Things'. However, because she cannot bear to have him out of her sight, she intends to go with him. What I want to highlight here is not just Steele's irony about the mother, but his scorn for her anxiety about her son: 'I could not but believe that this Humour of carrying a Boy to Travel in his Mother's Lap . . . is a Case of an extraordinary Nature, and carries on it a particular Stamp of Folly.' In his 'Essay on education', Jonathan Swift drew a scathing portrait of the mother who coddles her son and expects his tutor to do the same: 'master must not walk till he is hot . . . nor be wet in his feet', nor must he be kept 'too long poring over his book, because he is subject to sore eyes, and of a weakly constitution' (1880: I, 291). Daniel Defoe blamed 'Lady mothers' for the indolence and deficiencies of the 'head of the Heir to the Estate whom they have "robb'd of his education" by keeping him at home in the nursery instead of letting him go to school' (1890 [1728]: 6). As the century advanced, the language of the comments became more virulent. John Littleton Costeker complained about the number of young gentlemen who 'have been deprived of all the Pleasures and Advantages of Education by the Prejudices of too great a Tenderness' from their 'Lady-Mothers':

> Thousands are ruined by this very Effect of a maternal Love. What Pity is it that a great and heroick Soul, formed by Nature for noble Actions as noble as its Birth, should be thus lost both to the World and to himself . . . through the Fear of its being injured by a Methodical Education and the Care and Assiduity of Praeceptors; his constitution is first ruined by Indulgence, his Genius left uncultivated, and himself deprived of all but a domestick Knowledge: and thus is our young Nobleman by being ignorant of the mor noble and politer Education of his own Sex, naturally under the Conduct and Tuition of his Mamma, becomes instead of a fine Scholar . . . a compleat Fop.
>
> (Costeker 1732: 9–10)

John Brown's most-cited jeremiad is about the 'vain, luxurious, and selfish Effeminacy' of the 'Character and Manners of our Times'. What is not usually included in the quote is that Brown traces this effeminacy to the 'unwholesome Warmth' of the nursery, a 'Fountain of Weakness and Disease', for it is where mothers exercise their 'mistaken Tenderness and Care' (1757: I, 30). Twenty years later, convinced that it was in the nursery that 'we often perceive . . . the embryos of those distorted beings called fops, fribbles and coxcombs', James Fordyce exhorted the 'Mothers of Britain':

> What a mighty task is yours! . . . How much have those of you to Answer for, whose fantastic fondness has, from the very days in which you ought to have laid the foundation of virtue and glory, entailed the corruption and dishonour on your offspring! How strangely different from the Mothers of Antiquity who, having bred their sons to everything Manly and heroic, were accustomed . . . to charge them either to come back victorious, or to be brought back dead, choosing that they should not live in shame.
>
> (Fordyce 1777: II, 160–2)

Why was the figure of the overfond mother positioned as a link between education and effeminacy? To appreciate the importance and significance of this link, it is necessary to situate it in the major eighteenth-century debate on education, the public/private debate. How should gentlemen's sons be educated: privately at home, or publicly at school? This debate, which John Locke put at the heart of his educational treatise, *Some Thoughts upon Education*, occupied the pens of many and divers writers throughout the century. Advocates of a private, domestic education claimed it promised virtue and good breeding, whereas advocates of a public, school education claimed it fostered emulation, manly assurance and an early knowledge of the world. In the first half of the century, supporters of private education conceded, like Locke, that boys bred 'like Fondlings' at home might evince an enervating 'sheepish softness' (Locke 1922 [1693]: §70, 50), but claimed that the protection from vice that home education guaranteed more than compensated for this disadvantage. Advocates of public education acknowledged that schools might encourage vicious habits, but maintained that the value of 'emulation' in the formation of character compensated for schools' possible failings. Some even suggested a 'third way' – a small group of boys under a private tutor – as a way of getting boys away from the home (Burgh 1754: 112–13), but this was not a significant part of the debate.

In the 1780s, the association of home-educated boys with sheepish softness was elaborated and shaped into a concern about effeminacy. Educationist Vicesimus Knox, Master of Tonbridge School, was a key figure in this shift. The representation of the domestic environment and its indulgences as being problematic for boys had long been thought a problem. James Burgh had put it bluntly: 'the sooner a boy is sent from home for his education, the better' (1754: 111). Advocates of public schooling exploited this concern to support their critique of domestic education. But Knox went further. Like Locke, Knox believed virtue ought to be the main aim of boys' education, but his plan for its attainment was entirely different. In direct opposition to Locke, Knox argued that domestic instruction, far from shielding youths from vice actually promoted it because home eduction was indulgent and lacking in discipline. Shifting the site of vice from the school to the home made it possible for Knox to shift the site of virtue from the home to the school, thereby subverting the basis of Locke's claim for the superiority of domestic education. For Knox, public schooling alone guaranteed the discipline necessary for virtue and manliness (Cohen 2004).

In other words, Knox constructed 'masculinity' as he enunciated the advantages of public schooling, and 'effeminacy' as he denounced domestic education. The figure of the overfond mother was the foundation upon which domestic education produced effeminacy. 'Boys of manly spirits are often broken down and rendered effeminate and contemptible, by too great a degree of parental solicitude . . . the boy who has been kept in leading strings too long . . . by the fondness of his mother, will never be a man; never possess that becoming spirit which can enable him to act his part with propriety' (Knox 1781: 288–9).

Placing gender at the heart of the debate opened up a space where moralists and educationists would manipulate the meanings of public and private to construct or reinforce gender difference. Thus, William Barrow, an educationist who endorsed many of Knox's perceptions and recommendations, could ridicule the 'delicate nursling of domestick education, who shivers at the approach of every shower, and consults his thermometer before he ventures into the open air' (Barrow 1802: I, 109). The only circumstance when a private education would be advisable was for boys whose physical or mental debility required that they be 'sheltered in glass houses' like tender plants, unlike the oak which flourishes best 'in an open exposure' (Knox 1781: 41–2; Barrow 1802: 110). Jane West, who published vast moral tomes at the turn of the century, brought the point home: she recommended a public education for boys because they were more likely to make 'not merely shining but valuable men' by being sent to school. The home-educated boy, she warned, was susceptible not just to ridicule, but,

> if he has had a very tender and assiduous mother . . . the timidity or effeminacy of his manners may cast a ridicule over his moral purity, which, when he comes to venture into mixed society, he will perhaps endeavour to obviate, not by the assumption of hardihood, but by the affectation, or even the practice, of vice.
>
> (West 1806: III, 222–3)

Domestic education was suitable, then, only for those who would never be men – 'weaklings, imbeciles' and, of course, girls.

What about girls? Mary Wollstonecraft worried about overfond mothers because their 'mistaken fondness or blind zeal' counteracted the 'wise designs of nature' and the child, 'particularly a girl, [is] thus rendered dependent – dependence is called natural' (1995 [1792]: 113, 243). Wollstonecraft was an exception. Most criticism of mothers concerned not excessive motherhood but its opposite, neglectful mothers, those whose fashionable life and amusements took them away from their maternal responsibilities. As a result of the popularisation of Rousseau's ideas from the 1760s, conduct and moral/educational literature called for women, especially in the upper classes, to engage in a more 'natural, time-intensive' motherhood (McCreary 2004: 187), and was replete with advice – and criticism – about the role of mothers in their daughters' education.

There was no public/private debate about girls' education equivalent to that for boys in the eighteenth century, in the main because educationists and moralists were unanimous that girls should be educated at home. However, despite, or because, of the growing popularity of boarding schools for girls in the late eighteenth century (Skedd 1997), the wrath of moralists and educationists was directed at mothers who sent daughters to these schools. The anxiety that this trend generated can be gauged by the emergence of a new genre of moral literature, letters between mothers and their daughters at boarding school. In these letters, the mother remains a good mother because she has an acceptable reason for sending her daughter away – a woman might have to accompany her husband to India (*The Governess* 1785) – and she makes sure her daughter knows that 'though you are removed from my sight you are not, for all that, banished from my thoughts. On the contrary, you are more in them now than ever' (Allen 1769: 1–2). The anxiety about schools also spawned various writings which demonstrated, in inflammatory prose, the 'pernicious effects of improper female education' (Corry 1803: 34): a boarding school education.

Moralists and educationists had long been ambivalent towards boarding schools, arguing that the education they purveyed was 'useless, and . . . pernicious' (Wray 1997 [1714]: 54). Although a mother could be represented as neglectful because she hired a fashionable (usually French), rather than a worthy, governess for her daughter's home education (Edgeworth 1848 [1802]), it was sending a daughter to a boarding school that became the measure of good mothering against bad, especially in the later part of the century. Parents 'who think themselves generous and liberal' in giving their daughters a public education are misguided, lamented Rev. John Bennett, since 'whatever elegant or high-sounding schools may be sought out for a girl, a mother seems the only governess intended by nature' (1787: 138). Boarding schools were said to impart 'false and useless ideas, habits of idleness, indifference, or extravagance' and to focus mainly or solely on 'external accomplishments', to neglect 'moral duties and social virtues' doing nothing to 'engage [girls'] attention and render it an employment of the mind' (Jardine 1788: I, 329; Reeve 1792: 183–4; Wollstonecraft 1787: 25). Critics' arguments intensified when comparing boys' and girls' education, drawing attention to the opposing aims of male and female education at the same time as they served to reinforce these differences.

Schools, emphasised one critic, allow boys to develop the assurance necessary to deal with the world, but also encourage girls to become 'self-assured, forward and impudent' and lose the qualities that 'form the characteristick Beauties of the Sex', especially 'Timidity – bashful Reserve – Tenderness – and Delicacy' (Foster 1779: 16). Bennett maintained that 'almost everything' in schools could 'corrupt the heart'. They were 'hot beds' forcing girls prematurely out of girlhood innocence and promoting forwardness and independence. It is 'a publick education which first inspires the rage for pleasure and dissipation', which 'undomesticates' a woman and therefore 'unmakes her as to all the valuable purposes of her existence' he vituperated (1787: 142–4). Home education alone guaranteed the delicacy and diffidence that were the essence of femininity, an essence encapsulated in the certainty that a home-educated girl would be unlikely to 'canvass for votes at an election' (Bennett 1789: II, 29). Above all, and this was a critical argument in view of the aims of education, while public schooling promised virtue for males, it threatened the virtue of females. Female virtue was 'a plant of too delicate a nature, to risk this scorching method of exposure' (Bennett 1787: 150).

Bennett was not alone in advocating public education for boys and opposing it for girls. Vicesimus Knox, who strongly supported women's education, also intervened in the debate:

> It has been asked, why I approve of public education for boys and not for girls, and whether the danger to boys in large seminaries is not as great as to girls? I must answer, in general, that the corruption of girls is more fatal in its consequences to society than that of boys; and that, as girls are destined to private and domestic life, and boys to public life, their education should be respectively correspondent to their destination. Vanity and vice will be introduced by some among a large number, and the contagion soon spreads with irresistible violence.
>
> (Knox 1789: I, 331)

Like Rev. John Bennett, Rev. Chirol considered that the general immorality and corruption of the age and the 'misconduct of women and their ignorance of their duties, their errors and dissipation' were attributable to boarding school education. But he did not stop there. Having listed the pernicious moral and physical dangers attendant on a boarding school education – immorality, ill-health and falling into 'secret indulgence', a vice which could lead to death – Chirol delivered the ultimate sentence: parents were guilty of 'criminal neglect' if they failed to bring daughters up 'beneath the parental roof' where they can grow up 'sound, healthy, and happy' (1809: xiii, xiv, 26, 44, 123, 175). The tenderness of a mother was a requirement, for 'the perfect intimacy between mothers and daughters, which is one of the most desirable objects in education . . . cannot possibly take place when children are separated from their parents, as they are in boarding schools' (ibid.: 123). This is why Chirol considered that sending a girl to boarding school was violating 'the sacred obligations parents owed their daughters'. Yet, with the exception of Mary Wollstonecraft (1995 [1792]), no-one in the eighteenth century ever worried about the possible loosening of affective familial ties for boys attending public school.

This overview of a problematised mother suggests that to historicise motherhood and the ways it is 'constantly being re-constructed within the context of historically-specific social and economic relations' (Woodward 1997: 251), requires us to recognise that motherhood was not a unitary concept. Particular strands of prescriptive literature even split the mother into the mother of the boy and the mother of the girl.

As I have shown in the preceding discussion, one of the more striking features of the construct of overfond motherhood is its gendered practice and effect. But there is another component of the concept, the crucial dimension of time. Overfondness, unlike other failures of motherhood, such as neglect or cruelty, is often invoked retrospectively, for though the ideal mother is expected to have perfect children, it is only in the children's future, adult, embodiment that the quality of their mothering will be judged. Richardson's *Clarissa* offers an interesting example of the interweaving of gender and time in the character of two overfond mothers, one of a daughter, Clarissa, and the other of a son, Lovelace. Clarissa's mother is accused by her husband of having been 'a too fond mother, who, from motives of blameable indulgence, encouraged a child to stand in opposition to a father's will'. In fact, Clarissa's mother complains that

> It is a grating thing . . . for the parents of a child, who delighted in her all the time of her helpless infancy, and throughout every stage of her childhood, and in every part of her education to womanhood, because of the promises she gave of proving the most grateful and dutiful of children; to find, just when the time arrived which should crown their wishes, that child . . . defies her family.
> (Richardson 1982 [1747/8]: I, 98)

It is Lovelace himself who blames his mother for bringing him up 'to bear no control'. 'Why', he writes in a letter to John Belford, 'was I so educated, *as that to my very tutors it was a request that I should not know what contradiction and disappointment was*? Ought she not to have known what cruelty there was in her kindness?' This maternal cruelty has left him vulnerable to the great punishment of having his 'first very great disappointment touch [his] intellect' (ibid.: I, 98; IV, 442–3). Thus, while maternal overfondness is invoked to explain why a daughter, Clarissa, has become headstrong and (unnaturally) resists paternal authority, it is deployed to explain how a son, Lovelace, is failing to meet moral and intellectual expectations. This gender difference has significant consequences.

Representations of the overfond mother appear to absolve sons from responsibility for adult failure to be virtuous and manly. Bowers argues that because Richardson assigns the blame for Lovelace's behaviour to his mother, she 'emerges as the initiator of all the novel's heartache, the one ultimately responsible for her son's criminality'. In a letter to Lady Braidshaigh, Richardson made clear this was his intention: 'Mr Lovelace's Mother is often hinted at in the Progress of the Story, as having by her faulty indulgence to him in his early Youth, been the Occasion of that uncontroulableness [*sic*] of Will, which proved so fatal to many Innocents and in the End to himself' (Bowers 1996: 218). Being dead before the novel begins, Lovelace's mother 'stands as the paradigm for a version of motherhood still influential today: the mother who is, by definition, entirely responsible, yet who is also almost entirely invisible' (ibid.).

Samuel Johnson painted an equally dark portrait of an overfond mother in a series of letters in *The Rambler*. Recounted by Eumathes, tutor to a young nobleman, these letters also describe a son who fails to realise his promise because of the overfondness of his mother. For the story to act as a cautionary tale, the time dimension must be reversed so that the progressive corruption of the overindulged boy is shown to be inevitable and predetermined. The rot sets in with the mother's disregard for her young son's studies. Ever ready to have him 'excused from his task' be it as 'reward for some petty compliance' or to exhibit him to visitors, she teaches him that 'every thing was more pleasing and more important than knowledge and that study was to be endured rather than chosen, and was only the business of those hours which pleasure left vacant'. Taken to London, the young gentleman quickly learns not the wisdom his tutor would have liked to impart, but the corrupting ways of the town. He is eventually disgraced and ashamed. What makes Johnson's portrayal of the mother particularly mordant is that when finally ready to admit that her son has dishonoured the whole family, 'touched with his tears' she fails to exert what Wollstonecraft calls 'enlightened maternal affection' (1995 [1792]: 243). She opposes the family decision to send the youth to the country for two years under the care of his tutor, and 'declares that she thought him too much of a man to be any longer confined to his book, and he therefore begins his travels to-morrow under a French tutor' – travel to the continent and French being signifiers of frivolity and effeminacy (Cohen 1992: 241–57). Johnson's overfond mother is not just misguided, she destroys any prospect of her son's redemption. Mothers, Johnson comments, have high expectations of their sons, because 'women always judge absurdly of the intellect of their boys' (*The Rambler* 1752, Letter 194). They have no such expectations of their daughters.

The representations of mothers of daughters are not as homogeneous as those of mothers of sons. Thus, Wollstonecraft's overfond mother renders her daughter dependent while Richardson's causes hers to be defiant and headstrong. But there is one feature which representations of mothers of daughters, overfond or negligent, all share: they serve as a means of disciplining women. Wollstonecraft thought 'it was time to effect a revolution in female manners – time to make [women], as a part of the human species, labour by reforming themselves to reform the world' (1995 [1792]: 117). 'Rightly educated', comments McKeon, 'the female child becomes the domestic wife and mother' who will act as model for the next generation (2005: 187). The correct mothering and education of daughters is easily depicted. Educationist Clara Reeve was convinced that the best teacher was a virtuous and well-informed mother who gave up her attention 'to dress, to visiting, to cards, and to public places' (1792: 112) to devote herself to her daughter. Mothers should be 'deeply concerned in the tuition, improvement and welfare' of their daughters; 'nothing which interests them, or affects their interest, can possibly be indifferent to you', John Moir advised the female readers of his popular *Female Tuition* (1800 [1794]: 59). Similarly, Chirol's mother provides 'vigilant inspection, enlightened care, and tender solicitude . . . and spares no time, no trouble, no expence [sic] to ensure her continual welfare' (Chirol 1809: 44–5). 'Tenderness', writes Bowers, 'is a key word for describing virtuous maternal sentiment and behaviour' (1996: 167).

25

What Bowers and other scholars have overlooked is that for boys this tenderness signalled danger. 'Maternal fondness in excess has often caused a favourite boy, who promised better things, to become at last what is called in the world a poor creature', lamented Knox (1781: 288). Since gender and time transform the mother into a Janus-like figure, the question is: when does the tenderness associated with virtuous motherhood become 'overfondness'? What constitutes the boundary which maternal tenderness transgresses?

Since a mother's devotion is dangerous when directed towards a son, does the disciplining apply? With regards to sons, it could be argued that the discipline of mothers is exerted in a more insidious and controlling manner. By the late eighteenth century, the 'maternal "instinct"' was increasingly invoked . . . to define woman's nature' (Poovey 1988: 7). Maternal sentiment was held to be so natural that Burton could declare in his lectures to girls at a boarding school, 'however strong . . . we may suppose the fondness of a Father for his Children, yet [we] will find more lively marks of tenderness in the bosom of a Mother' (1793: I, 93–4). At the same time as the naturalness of maternal sentiment was normalised, solutions were elaborated to forestall the effects of its excess. In his *Essay upon Nursing*, the physician William Cadogan had already challenged the implicit authority conferred on mothers by their nursing of infants, warning that it was a 'business too long fatally left to the management of women' as demonstrated in the cases where the 'Heir and Hope of the family . . . dies a victim to the mistaken care and tenderness of his fond mother' (1748: 3). Invested with the power not only of life but also of death, mothers must be reigned in through the authority of a male expert (Alyea 1998).

While mothers of daughters could be regulated and disciplined into the idealised figures imagined by moralists and educationists, could mothers ever be ideal mothers of sons? In a sense, late eighteenth-century English culture said 'no'. In the nineteenth century, it was the public school, which, as *loco parentis*, would increasingly represent the ideal parent. In the twentieth century, the image of the overfond mother as dangerous to her son was still significant enough for an advertisement in *The Times* in 1944 to ask 'Is this mother dangerous?' The picture shows a mother, her son and her daughter, but the caption refers only to the son (Heward 1988: 179). Thus, while the eighteenth century produced a solicitous, devoted, selfless and tender 'natural' mother, this representation could sustain in relation to daughters but not to sons. All the traits that constituted the mother's idealised persona were translated into ways of damaging and emasculating sons, for whom she represented not mother but (s)mother.

Note

1 See, however, Lee Davidoff and Catherine Hall (1987) *Family Fortunes: Men and women of the English middle class, 1780–1850.* London: Hutchinson.

References

Allen, C. (1769) *The Polite Lady or a Course of Female Education in a Series of Letters from a Mother to a Daughter*. London.

Alyea, C. (1998) 'Dress, childhood, and the modern body: the body politics of children's dress reform in eighteenth-century Europe'. Unpublished PhD thesis, Harvard University.

Barrow, William (1802) *An Essay on Education*, 2 vols. London.

Bennett, John (1787) *Strictures on Female Education; Chiefly in Relation to the Culture of the Heart*. London.

— (1789) *Letters to a Young Lady on Useful and Interesting Subjects Calculated to Improve the Heart, to Form the Manners, and Enlighten the Understanding*, 2 vols. Dublin.

Bowers, T. (1996) *The Politics of Motherhood: British writing and culture, 1680–1760*. Cambridge: Cambridge University Press.

Brown, J. (1757) *An Estimate of the Manners and Principles of the Time*, 2 vols. London.

Burgh, J. (1754) *The Dignity of Human Nature*. London.

Burton, J. (1793) *Lectures on Female Education and Manners*, 2 vols. London.

Cadogan, William (1748) *Essay upon Nursing*. London.

Chirol, J.L. (1809) *An Enquiry into the Best System of Female Education; or Boarding School and Home Education Attentively Considered*. London.
Cohen, M. (1992) 'The Grand Tour: constructing the English gentleman in eighteenth century France'. *History of Education*, 21(3), 241–57.
— (2004) 'Gender and the private/public debate on education in the long eighteenth century'. In R. Aldrich (ed.) *Public or Private Education? Lessons from history*. London: Woburn Press.
Corry, J. (1803) *The Unfortunate Daughter: Or, the danger of the modern system of education*. London.
Costeker, J.L. (1732) *The Fine Gentleman or the Complete Education of a Young Nobleman*. London.
Davidoff, L. and Hall, C. (1987) *Family Fortunes: Men and women of the English middle class, 1780–1850*. London: Hutchinson.
Defoe, D. (1890) *The Compleat English Gentleman* [1728] (ed. K.D. Bülbring). London: David Nutt.
Edgeworth, M. (1848) *Mademoiselle Panache* [1802]. London: Longman.
Fordyce, James (1777) *Addresses to Young Men*, 2 vols. London.
Foster, F. (1779) *Thoughts on the Times but Chiefly on the Profligacy of our Women*. London.
Gildon, C. and Brightland, J. (1967) *A Grammar of the English Tongue* [1711]. Menston: Scolar Press.
The Governess, or the Boarding School Dissected (1785). London.
Heward, C. (1988*) Making a Man of Him: Parents and their sons' education at an English public school, 1929–50*. London: Routledge.
Jardine, A. (1788) *Letters from Barbary, France, Portugal, etc.*, 2 vols. London.
Knox, Vicesimus (1781 and 1789) *Liberal Education or, A Practical Treatise on the Methods of Acquiring Useful and Polite Learning*, 2 vols. London.
Locke, J. (1922) 'Some Thoughts upon Education' [1693], in J.W. Adamson (ed.) *The Educational Writings of John Locke*. Cambridge: Cambridge University Press.
McCreary, C. (2004) *The Satirical Gaze: Prints of women in late eighteenth-century England*. Oxford: Clarendon.
McKeon, M. (2005) *The Secret History of Domesticity: Public, private, and the division of knowledge*. Baltimore, MD: Johns Hopkins University Press.
Moir, John (1800) *Female Tuition, or an Address to Mothers* [1784]. London.
Poovey, M. (1988) *Uneven Developments: The ideological work of gender in mid-Victorian England*. London: University of Chicago Press.
The Rambler, a periodical paper published by Samuel Johnson (1750–2).

Reeve, C. (1792) *Plans of Education*. London.

Richardson, S. (1982) *Clarissa or The History of a Young Lady* [1747/8]. Everyman's Library, 4 vols. London: Dent.

Skedd, S. (1997) 'Women teachers and the expansion of girls' schooling in England, c.1760–1820'. In H. Barker and C. Chalus (eds) *Gender in Eighteenth-century England*. London: Longman.

Stone, L. (1977) *The Family, Sex and Marriage 1500–1800*. London: Weidenfeld and Nicolson.

Swift, J. (1880) 'An essay on modern education'. In T. Roscoe (ed.) *The Works of Jonathan D.D. Swift*, 2 vols. London: Geo. Bell & Sons.

The Spectator, a periodical paper published by Joseph Addison and Richard Steele (1711–14).

Trumbach, R. (1978) *The Rise of the Egalitarian Family: Aristocratic kinship and domestic relations in eighteenth-century England*. New York: Academic Press.

West, Jane (1806) *Letters to a Young Lady*, 3 vols. London.

Wilson, Thomas (1729) *The Many Advantages of a Good Language to Any Nation*. London.

Wollstonecraft, M. (1787) *Thoughts on the Education of Daughters, with Reflections on Female Conduct, in the More Important Duties of Life*. London.

— (1995) *A Vindication of the Rights of Woman* [1792] (ed. S. Tomaselli). Cambridge: Cambridge University Press.

Woodward, K. (1997) 'Motherhood: identities, meanings and myths'. In K. Woodward (ed.) *Identity and Difference*. London: Sage.

Wray, M. (1997) 'The Ladies Library' [1714], cited in D. Raftery, *Women and Learning in English Writing, 1600–1900*. Dublin: Four Courts Press.

2 Educational policy-making: economic and historical perspectives

Vincent Carpentier

Introduction

It will be argued in this chapter that increased emphasis on economic perspectives can offer historians of education new theoretical and methodological tools and also broaden understandings of policy-making. The potential for economics to colonise other social sciences presents a danger, however (Fine and Green 2000), so what is proposed here is a combination, rather than a merger, of perspectives designed to analyse the relationship between public expenditure on education and economic cycles. The complexity of this has been acknowledged in Richard Aldrich's *Education for the Nation*, which notes that 'education may serve either as a means of investment, or of consumption' (1996: 130). Other examples of Aldrich's writing (e.g. Aldrich *et al.* 2000) have highlighted a complex and inconsistent relationship between education and the economy; one that has been influenced strongly by historical change over time and the objectives of the State.

The economy, history and education

While not altogether ignoring the issue, historians of education have sometimes integrated economic contexts into their writings with reluctance. The economy tends to be presented as an environment, but its impact on both the conception and implementation of education policy is rarely explored in depth, even though the financial resourcing of policy initiatives, schools and classrooms has been – and continues to be – a significant influence upon teaching and learning. Pragmatic encounters between economic and educational historians have produced some important outcomes. In 1997, for example, a British History of Education Society conference generated a special journal issue on the theme of education and economic performance (Lowe and McCulloch 1998). More recently, Michael Sanderson has called for bridge building between the two fields (2005).

In the 1940s, as Gary McCulloch has observed, Fred Clarke called for an 'interpretation, conscious and deliberate, of education in terms of a social economic history' (quoted in McCulloch 2004: 8), and the work of one British historian of education, above all others, confirms a commitment to this objective. The writings of Brian Simon (1915–2002) examine educational and social change through a Marxist lens, focusing on social class within broader economic structures. This implies recognition of, though not an allegiance to, the economic perspective. On the one hand, Simon argues that 'the fundamental educational issues have remained the same through the years – who should be educated, how, to what level or different levels of the service of what social or industrial needs? – so the conditioning social and economic factors continue to operate' (Simon 1966: 70). On the other hand, Simon criticised 'reproduction theories' associated with Bourdieu and Bowles and Gintis because they failed to recognise education's 'degree of relative autonomy' from 'the economic structure' (Brehony 2004: 546).

The application of economic theory to educational examples has been tentative. Classical economists associated education with political and social stability, creating favourable conditions for economic development. Adam Smith (1776) envisaged a direct relationship between education and economic performance by comparing a skilled worker to an expensive machine, but it was more than a century before Alfred Marshall developed an economic model that embraced education. Marshall (1890) viewed education as an investment of individuals in themselves in order to transform the type of labour supplied. This may be seen as an attempt to bring economic rationality to the concept of education.

This challenge was next taken up in the 1960s, when human capital theory treated education as a constituent element of rational economic choice. Just like physical capital, the quantity and level of education to be provided rested upon microeconomic decision-making: the costs of individuals' education were balanced by the benefits of their increased productivity, rewarded by higher wages (Becker 1962). A transposition of this model to the macroeconomic level established a direct and positive link between national educational investment and national income. Abandoning the previous assumption of homogeneous labour shifted the focus towards the qualitative factors of economic growth: knowledge came to be seen as the main driving force of the economy (Romer 1990).

Economic theory has been shown to be both reactive and proactive vis-à-vis educational policy-making. Human capital theory emphasised the contribution of education to economic growth, as revealed by empirical studies (e.g. Denison 1967), but it also endorsed the post-Second World War programme of public investment in education. The education system could be represented not only as a cost for the economic system, but also as an investment and major determinant of growth. This balanced view was to change after the 1973 oil crisis hastened the end of the post-war consensus. The tax burden associated with education was now widely thought to outweigh the benefits. In part, this was because the financial costs and levels of visible taxation, used as indicators by policy-makers, seemed straightforward in comparison with the harder-to-measure outputs showing economic benefits.

In the process of investigating the factors behind economic growth, economists have gradually given more space to education, but have tended to understand it in a narrow way. According to John Vaizey, this was one reason why Marshall did not pursue his exploration of human capital and education (Vaizey 1972: 22). It can be argued, therefore, that the disciplinary shift from *political economy*, a social science uniting politics and economics, towards *economic science*, with its emphasis upon the alternative uses of scarce resources by individuals and societies, has refined the theoretical relationship between education and economic growth, while sidelining the indirect economic benefits attached to education, as identified by classical economists. Something has been lost here: the history of educational policy-making may better be understood if we locate policy dilemmas, past and present, in a context that recognises prevailing economic conditions.

In the United Kingdom, debates have centred around the historical links between education and economic growth. Did education contribute to the first industrial revolution and the economic hegemony that followed? Is the lack of education before the second industrial revolution of the late nineteenth century responsible for the economic decline of the twentieth (Aldcroft 1974; Sanderson 1999)? If so, was this inevitable (McCloskey 1970)? Such debates have been coloured by historians' own perspectives on public versus private education, another strong research interest of Richard Aldrich (2004). Some have presented public intervention as a wrong move, or mistake, which permanently destabilised the progress towards educational development begun by efficient private institutions (e.g. West 1975). By contrast, others see public education as a necessary response to socio-economic problems ignored by private organisations (e.g. Simon 1960: 115; Anderson 1983). The hazards of drawing comparisons across time, of straying into counterfactual 'what if' territory, and of attempting to disaggregate the contribution of education from other cultural, social and political factors that may have affected economic development are legion. But historians of education have been culpable of underestimating the influence of economic forces upon the settings they are studying, tending to follow debates rather than leading them. For example, William Richardson (1999: 131) regrets that there has been no significant engagement by historians of education with the highly contentious thesis about the failure of British education to serve the needs of industry, set out in Martin Wiener's (1981) volume *English Culture and the Decline of the Industrial Spirit.*

Alternative explanations of the relationship between education and the State also reflect competing methodologies. Questions arise about the reliability and availability of quantitative data for such issues as enrolment, literacy rates and expenditure (West 1970; Hurt 1971), while qualitative studies of, for example, curriculum, pedagogy and values present difficulties for comparing past and present. Today's policy-makers continue to face timeless questions. What is education for? How should it be evaluated? This chapter provides no answers to those questions, but it does argue that the combination of method-ologies is crucial to define, evaluate and interpret the quantitative and qualitative development of educational systems. This, in turn, is an aid to better understanding the similarities and differences across time and space.

Three main developments are considered below: first, the relation-ship between economic fluctuations, educational funding and policy; second, comparisons between education and other areas of State activity; and, finally, international comparisons.

Long economic cycles and education policies

It is argued here that paying close attention to long economic cycles, or 'Kondratiev waves', can illuminate the historical relation-ship between British education, the State and the economy. Nikolai Kondratiev (1892–1938), the Russian economist, argued that Western capitalist states experience regular cycles of boom followed by depres-sion (Louçã and Reijnders 1999). A study of fluctuations in educational funding since 1833 (see Figure 2.1) shows that, since the first public

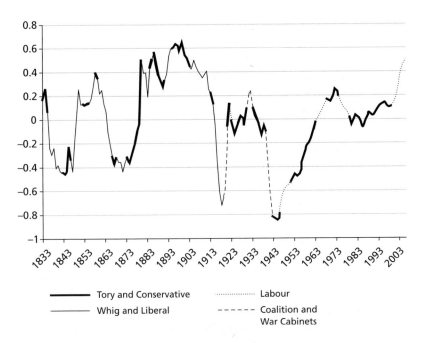

Figure 2.1 UK public expenditure on education (1990 prices), 1833–2005 (second order deviation from the regression curve)

Source: Carpentier (2001) (updated).

grant to education was made in that year, the 'highs' and the 'lows' of educational activity are in reverse to the Kondratiev waves prior to 1945, but are synchronised thereafter (Carpentier 2003). One interpretation, therefore, is that the Second World War fundamentally changed the relationship between education and economic growth.

Before 1945, periods of economic boom resulted from cost savings, including a slowdown in education spending. Evidence points to such policies contributing to economic upturns in the short term, but in the longer term they tend to generate lower levels of productivity and to increase social unrest. This leads to a crisis of capital, which, though it may be abundant, is not invested efficiently. Increasing

35

public spending on education forms part of the solution to overcome such crises: unused capital is deployed to restore labour productivity and a long-term dynamic of profit. Contrary to the thesis of E.G. West, this explanation suggests that nineteenth-century State involvement in education was the result, not the cause, of economic setbacks (West 1975; Carpentier 2003).

After 1945, the preconditions of growth changed. They were no longer based on lowering the cost of the factors of production, but derived instead from qualitative improvements. From this point, public expenditure on education became a conscious instrument of the post-war economic growth (Michel 1999). But this situation was to change again with the onset of the early 1970s' world oil crisis, which precipitated cuts in public spending and hastened the end of the post-war consensus (Chitty 2004: 16).

Such an interpretation should be treated with caution, not least because certain economists are sceptical about the existence and significance of cycles (e.g. Solomou 1987). Some historians, meanwhile, feel uneasy about associating cyclical analysis with historical determinism, repetition and prediction. Yet analyses of this kind can be valuable as long as we recognise that cycles are of different amplitudes and periodicities, and that they illustrate the *recurrence of mechanisms*, rather than the *reproduction of identical situations*. What does seem clear is that long-term economic fluctuations are likely to be affected by – and may themselves influence – public spending on education. Cyclical analysis cannot explain the whole process of educational development, but it does go some way towards responding to Eric Hobsbawm's call for historians to collaborate with economists to better understand socio-economic transformation (1997: 163).

In respect of the UK, Table 2.1 offers a brief interpretation of the upward and downward phases of long economic cycles and the development and funding of education. While there are correlations here, these do not automatically signify causality. As McCulloch has argued, educational history 'can provide a testing ground, the test of time for the relationship between education and economic performance'

Table 2.1 Phases of long economic cycles and the development and funding of education in the UK

Long cycles	Upward phases	Downward phases
1790–1850	c.*1790*–c.*1820* Economic advances of the 'first industrial revolution' occurred in spite of, not because of, educational provision. No state funding of education in this period.	c.*1820*–c.*1850* Economic instability and social unrest, yet the state began to fund elementary schooling (from 1833), develop a bureaucracy and establish a schools inspectorate.
1850–97	c.*1850*–c.*1873* A 'golden age' for the Victorian economy, but the Newcastle Report (1861) slowed educational spending and introduced 'payment by results' for schools.	c.*1873*–c.*1897* Marked by the 'First Great Depression', but a substantial rise in educational funding followed the 1870 Education Act. Elementary education subsequently became compulsory (1880) and free (1891).
1897–1945	c.*1897*–c.*1914* A modest economic recovery, but the 1902 Education Act was not accompanied by increased public investment.	c.*1914*–c.*1945* The Wall Street Crash (1929) and Great Depression impacted less severely on education spending than on other public spending.
1945–present	c.*1945*–c.*1973* Post-war economic growth was partly driven by universal secondary education and the expansion of higher education.	c.*1973*–present Economic turmoil led to the 'capture of education', with budget reductions and the State's partial retreat in favour of increased private resourcing.

(1998: 204). Even so, such test results may do little more than confirm a need for further enquiry and open-mindedness. In 1997, Richard Aldrich's contemporary, Roy Lowe, a contributor to this volume (Chapter 7), voiced doubts about the impact of education upon the economy, while simultaneously citing the Kondratiev wave theory as a possible explanation of the 1970s budget cuts (1997: 25).

The relationship between education and the economy is an evolving construct, potentially subject to continuity as well as change. Indeed, Richard Aldrich has questioned whether the 'discontinuity, disruption and chaos in the 1970s, 1980s and 1990s are any greater than during previous periods of history' (2006: 31). Acknowledging the cyclical recurrence of economic crises offers the reassurance of a pattern. The reversal of the relationship between education and the economy after the Second World War, however, presents a challenge for policy-makers. Received wisdom, since the 1970s, has been that public spending, including that devoted to education, must be restrained during periods of economic slowdown. Prior to 1945, however, evidence suggests not only that public expenditure on education *increased* during periods of economic crisis, but also that it provided a way out of the crisis.

The study of economic cycles is not a substitutive tool, but rather an additional lens available to historians of education policy. It presents a critique, supported by critical researchers (e.g. Ozga 2000: 118), of older, 'Whiggish' explanations, which view the development of State education as natural growth or as a pathway to progress, marked by legislative milestones. Cyclical analysis also challenges oversimplified associations between politics and education. Figure 2.1 shows, for example, that the party political transitions of governments do not necessarily lead to new patterns of economic spending. New governments initially find themselves locked into economic cycles, and while neither politics nor economics is the slave of the other, like the proverbial oil tanker, there can be a significant time lag before a decision to change the course of policy becomes manifest by a new direction in the expenditure statistics. Moreover, raw figures showing expenditure on education may be a blunt instrument for policy analysis. Prime ministers James Callaghan (Labour, 1976–9) and Margaret Thatcher (Conservative, 1979–90) were both associated with parsimony and the achievement of efficiencies in education, yet the 'wasted years' policy legacy of the former contrasts markedly with the 'revolution' associated with Thatcher's education reforms. 'Value for money', upon which governments have purported to focus since the early 1970s, has proved to be a misleading slogan. Most frequently, education initiatives are presented in a way that makes it easy to count the monetary cost, while an estimation of the policy's value is much less clear. The challenges of identifying and evaluating educational outputs are at the core of the Atkinson Report (2005) on public service productivity. But the lessons of history suggest that presenting education, and other public services, as an aggregation of costs will generate spreadsheet figures that fail to reflect the true value and public benefit. Cyclical analysis helps us to understand when, and possibly why, more funding is applied to education, but this quantitative approach is blind to qualitative data. In this respect, history of education adds a vital dimension: working together, economists and historians are better placed to understand the relationship between educational funding and policy development than either discipline can independently claim.

Cyclical analysis illustrates both education's dependence upon, and autonomy from, the economy. Two observations are important here. The first is that the expansion and development of education over time has been regularly justified as a precondition of economic growth. In spite of the poor health of the economy, there was a strong pattern of public investment in education, evidenced by the graphical peaks in the opening, mid-century and final years of Queen Victoria's monarchy and during the world economic depression of the 1930s. The second observation is that the 1973 oil crisis heralded the 'capture' of education by economics. From this point it became more difficult for the stakeholders of education, including the Department of Education and Science and its successors, to secure resources for initiatives that were not clearly related to economic performance.

Education, the public sector and the economy

Another benefit of engaging with the economic perspective is to facilitate comparisons between education and other State-funded activities. To what extent is the funding of education independent from, or subject to, the variables of other claims on the public purse?

Fontvieille (1976) observed a correlation between global public expenditure and economic cycles in France. Applying his methodology to the UK situation over an extended period demonstrates a similar outcome, as shown in Figure 2.2. In the UK, too, a significant increase in all public resources after the Second World War slowed in the early 1970s. At that point, stagflation – the combination of inflation and stagnation – undermined the Keynesian consensus and ushered in neo-

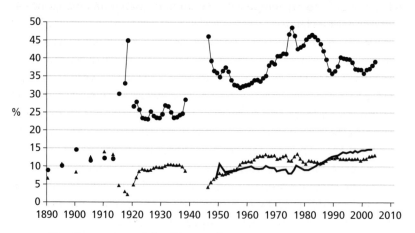

—▲— Education as a share of all public expenditure
—●— All public expenditure as a share of GDP
——— NHS spending as a share of all public expenditure

Figure 2.2 UK education and other public expenditure as a share of Gross Domestic Product (GDP), 1890–2004

Source: Carpentier (2001); Peacock and Wiseman (1994); Webster (1998) (updated).

liberal policies designed to fight inflation, such as wage control and public expenditure restraint. Public funding, not only in education, synchronised with Kondratiev fluctuations in the 1970s; but there are, nevertheless, characteristics of education that are distinct from other public activities.

Fontvieille made a distinction between the State's *regalian* spending (on, for example, national security and the maintenance of law) and those areas of expenditure linked to human development (including education, housing, health and social services). He identified a clearer historical pattern in the latter type of expenditure, with dynamic growth occurring during downward economic phases. Cyclical movements of global public funding, he concluded, were more predominantly driven by fluctuations of social expenditure than by regalian spending. Other French studies have confirmed this pattern and have pointed to similarities between the cyclical fluctuation of funding for health and education (Fontvieille 1990; Domin 2000). In the UK, evidence for the pre-1945 period certainly points to relatively high spending on health, education and housing at times of overall economic weakness. A study of health policy since 1939 (Berridge 1999), reflecting the shift from private and voluntarist initiatives to a National Health Service (NHS), suggests possibilities for further research to compare and contrast the expenditure fluctuations of education with other public spending on social welfare activities.

It is common for levels of government expenditure on education to be cited as a reflection of State ambitions and priorities for the area. But the full picture is likely to be more complex than this. Education is in competition for finite resources with other central government departments, with each of them likely to be thwarted by overall public-spending round caps and subject to the constraints of State taxation approaches that accompany neo-liberal agendas. Figure 2.2 offers mixed messages in respect of the relationship between education and total public spending. On the one hand, this shows how all public expenditure, including that on education, is affected by economic fluctuations. The trajectory of the line showing education as a share of all public expenditure after 1945 tells a different story: at the beginning of this period education claimed only a 5 per cent share, but in 1977 it reached the heights of 12 per cent, before stagnating in the recession of the late 1970s. Figure 2.2 further shows that education funding improved relative to expenditure on the NHS between the mid-1950s and the early 1970s, but then experienced a narrowing advantage before health claimed a higher percentage share from the 1990s.

At the heart of all public-sector spending discussions lie questions of whether the amount spent is too little or too much, and whether the sums granted are being spent efficiently. Yet the potential *value* of pursuing education policies may differ from the *costs*, judged in monetary terms. In the early 1860s, for example, as Richard Aldrich has shown, Sir John Pakington was hopeful that the work of the Newcastle Commission would herald an ambitious national education policy for the working classes. Such hopes evaporated with the Revised Code of 1862, introducing budget cuts and 'payment by results' (Aldrich 2006: 60). It was the absence of any recognition of education's qualitative measures in the Revised Code that underpinned the criticisms of Joseph Payne, the subject of another biographical study by Aldrich (ibid.: 103). A possible parallel may be drawn between this nineteenth-century era and the experience of the post-1980s education quasi-market. The budget slowdowns in this period are demonstrated by statistics, but, as with the Revised Code, qualitative improvements in educational provision were less evident (Campbell *et al.* 2003).

What becomes clear from this analysis is that, against a background of economic cycles, expenditure on education is autonomous, but it is influenced by variables that affect the public funding of other social activities too. Interdisciplinary approaches to educational research can deliver powerful lessons for policy-makers, and where research-informed practices can demonstrate positive synergies between social activities there may be a compelling case to break with the tradition of requiring one government department to compete for funding against another. For example, studies of health and education point to a 'virtuous circle': individuals with higher levels of education take better care of their health, and those in good health produce the best outcomes in the education system (Bynner and Feinstein 2005). On their own, economic statistics tell a partial story, but so, too, do narrow historical accounts. The potential for economists and historians to learn from each other in explaining educational change is considerable.

Educational resources and international perspectives

This chapter has focused mostly on the UK, but current debates about globalisation encourage us to consider whether transformations of particular kinds – economic, cultural, political and social – are always likely to impact upon education in the same way, or whether there are country-specific variables.

Figure 2.3, for example, suggests that for most of the past 130 years France, the UK and the USA have devoted similar percentages of gross domestic product (GDP) to educational spending, but also that there were significant differences in these countries' relative efforts at particular points in time.

The relationship between British public expenditure on education and economic cycles is consistent with the conclusions of previous studies in France (Fontvieille 1990) and the USA (Carpentier 2006a). In the UK, the period immediately following the 1870 Education Act was characterised by efforts to 'catch up' with economic competitors by 'filling up the gaps' in elementary education. The second industrial revolution of this period was more dependent than the first on knowledge and skills (Freeman and Louçã 2001). The higher levels of public funding for education in France and the USA might be attributed to conscious policies for the development of human capital, but other cultural, social and political forces may have been at work, too (see Green 1990; Bowles and Gintis 2002). Another turning point comes in the early 1970s, when the end of the international post-war consensus

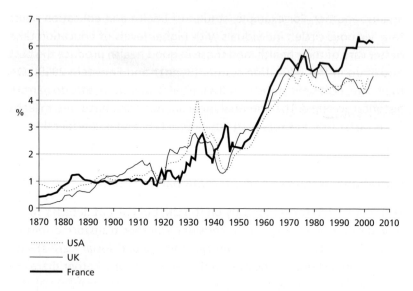

Figure 2.3 Public expenditure on education as a share of GDP, 1870–2003

Source: Carry (1999); Carpentier (2003, 2006a).

interrupted the rising trend of public funding for education. In the UK and USA, this led to increased marketisation and a rise in the levels of private resources (Carpentier 2006b). By contrast, such reforms have impacted much less on France, where a new dynamic of public expenditure on education gained momentum in the early 1990s.

Once more, there is a research agenda here for economists and historians to pursue collaboratively. The three countries represented in Figure 2.3 committed broadly similar percentages of national income to education during the first 100 years represented on the graph. Even where the lines become volatile and divergent, during the interwar period, the trend in each of these countries was to commit relatively *more*, rather than less, money to education. Does this constitute a framework or model – a Western one, at least – for understanding educational expansion? Similarly, there may be scope for economists and historians to examine whether the kinds of post-1973 national patterns shown in Figure 2.3 are consistent with, or challenge, theories of globalisation and understandings of how global forces may impact upon education. The various – and sometimes contradictory – messages from such international agencies as the International Monetary Fund, the World Bank and the Organisation for Economic Cooperation and Development concerning international education resource levels and targets are ripe for discussion and critique from educational historians, as well as economists of education. Similarly, the apparent trend, at an international level, for voluntary and private stakeholders to be involved with – and to finance – public education demands the engagement of historians if we are to learn lessons from past enterprises of this kind.

Conclusion

This chapter has sought to illustrate how the expansion of education has been both dependent upon, but also autonomous from, economics. Three main conclusions are offered here. The first is that quantitative and cyclical analysis reveals a relationship between the rhythmic pulsation of the economy and public expenditure on education. A next step should be for economists and historians to use quantitative and qualitative approaches to examine more closely the *impact* of such funding, in respect of national economic and educational development, and paying attention to such factors as student achievement, teachers' professional standing and pedagogical practices. The second conclusion is that, although public education has developed in a distinct manner, it operates alongside other publicly funded spheres. These areas are frequently advantaged or disadvantaged collectively, according to the State's overall public spending budget. But such areas as health and housing may also be in direct competition for limited public resources. Finally, national policies for educational expenditure may be influenced by globalisation, but there is scope for much more comparative and collaborative research in this area.

Acknowledgement

I am grateful to my colleague Dr David Crook for his comments and advice on an earlier draft of this chapter.

References

Aldcroft, D.H. (1974) 'McCloskey on Victorian growth: a comment'. *Economic History Review*, 27(2), 271–4.

Aldrich, R. (1996) *Education for the Nation*. London: Cassell.

— (ed.) (2004) *Private or Public Education? Lessons from history*. London: Woburn Press.

— (2006) *Lessons from History of Education: The Selected Works of Richard Aldrich*. London: Routledge.

Aldrich, R., Crook, D. and Watson, D. (2000) *Education and Employment: The DfEE and its place in history*. London: Institute of Education.

Anderson, R.D. (1983) 'Education and the State in nineteenth-century Scotland'. *Economic History Review*, 36(4), 518–34.

Atkinson, T. (2005) *Improvements in the Methodology for Measuring Government Output* (Atkinson Report). London: Office for National Statistics.

Becker, G.S. (1962) 'Investment in human capital: a theoretical analysis'. *Journal of Political Economy*, 70(5), 9–49.

Berridge, V. (1999) *Health and Society in Britain since 1939*. Cambridge: Cambridge University Press.

Bowles, S. and Gintis, H. (2002) 'Schooling in capitalist America revisited'. *Sociology of Education*, 75(1), 1–18.

Brehony, K. (2004) 'Education as a "social function": sociology, and social theory in the histories of Brian Simon'. *History of Education*, 33(5), 545–58.

Bynner, J. and Feinstein, L. (2005) 'What can policy learn from the research on the wider benefits of learning?'. *London Review of Education*, 3(3), 177–90.

Campbell, C., Carpentier, V. and Whitty, G. (2003) 'Educational financing and improvement: conceptual issues and policy debates in the UK'. *Revue Suisse des Sciences de l'Education*, 3, 455–77.

Carpentier, V. (2001) *Système Éducatif et Performances Économiques au Royaume-Uni: 19ème et 20ème siècles*. Paris: L'Harmattan.

— (2003) 'Public expenditure on education and economic growth in the UK, 1833–2000'. *History of Education*, 32(1), 1–15.

— (2006a) 'Public expenditure on education and economic growth in the USA in the nineteenth and twentieth centuries in comparative perspective'. *Paedagogica Historica*, 42(6), 683–706.

— (2006b) 'Funding in higher education and economic growth in France and the United Kingdom, 1921–2003'. *Higher Education Management and Policy*, 18(3), 1–26.

Carry, A. (1999) 'Le compte satellite rétrospectif de l'éducation en France: 1820–1996'. *Economies et Sociétés*, Série AF, Histoire quantitative de l'économie française, 25.

Chitty, C. (2004) *Education Policy in Britain*. Basingstoke: Palgrave Macmillan.

Denison, E.F. (1967) *Why Growth Rates Differ: Post-war experience in nine Western countries*. Washington, DC: The Brookings Institution.

Domin, J.P. (2000) 'Evolution et croissance de longue période du système hospitalier français: 1803–1993'. *Economies et Sociétés*, Série AF, Histoire économique quantitative, 26, 71–133.

Fine, B. and Green, F. (2000) 'Economics, social capital, and the colonization of the social sciences'. In S. Baron, J. Field and T. Schuller (eds) *Social Capital*. Oxford: Oxford University Press.

Fontvieille, L. (1976) 'Evolution et croissance de l'Etat français 1815–1969'. *Economies et Sociétés*, Cahiers de l'I SMEA, Série AF, 13, 1657–2149.

— (1990) 'Education, growth and long cycles: the case of France in the 19th and 20th centuries'. In G. Tortella (ed.) *Education and Economic Development since the Industrial Revolution*. Valencia: Generalitat Valenciana.

Freeman, C. and Louçã, F. (2001) *As Time Goes By*. Oxford: Oxford University Press.

Green, A. (1990) *Education and State Formation: The rise of education systems in England, France and the USA*. London: Macmillan.

Hobsbawm, E.J. (1997) *On History*. London: Abacus.

Hurt, J.S. (1971) 'Professor West on early nineteenth-century education'. *Economic History Review*, 24, 624–32.

Louçã, F. and Reijnders, J. (eds) (1999) *The Foundations of Long Wave Theory*. Cheltenham: Edward Elgar.

Lowe, R. (1997) *Schooling and Social Change, 1964–1990*. London: Routledge.

Lowe, R. and McCulloch, G. (eds) (1998) 'Education and economic performance'. *History of Education*, 27(3), special issue.

McCloskey, D.N. (1970) 'Did Victorian Britain fail?'. *Economic History Review*, 23(3), 446–59.

McCulloch, G. (1998) 'Education and economic performance'. *History of Education*, 27(3), 202–6.

— (2004) *Education, History and Social Change: The legacy of Brian Simon*. London: Institute of Education.

Marshall, A. (1890) *Principles of Economics* (reprinted 1961). New York: Macmillan.

Michel, S. (1999) *Education et Croissance Économique en Longue Période*. Paris: L'Harmattan.

Ozga, J. (2000) *Policy Research in Educational Settings*. Buckingham: Open University Press.

Peacock, A.T. and Wiseman, J. (1994) *The Growth of Public Expenditure in the United Kingdom*. London: Oxford University Press.

Richardson, W. (1999) 'Historians and educationists: the history of education as a field of study in post-war England Part II: 1972–96'. *History of Education*, 28(2), 109–41.

Romer, P.M. (1990) 'Endogenous technological change'. *Journal of Political Economy*, 98(5), S71–S102.

Sanderson, M. (1999) *Education and Economic Decline in Britain, 1870 to the 1990s*. Cambridge: Cambridge University Press.

— (2005) 'The history of education and economic history'. Paper presented at the University of Exeter, March.

Simon, B. (1960) *Studies in the History of Education (1780–1870)*. London: Lawrence and Wishart.

— (1966) 'The history of education'. In P. Gordon and R. Szreter (eds) (1989) *History of Education: The making of a discipline*. London: Woburn Press.

Smith, A. (1776) *An Enquiry into the Nature and Causes of the Wealth of Nations. Volume 1*. London: Methuen.

Solomou, S. (1987) *Phases of Economic Growth, 1850–1973: Kondratieff waves and Kuznets swings*. Cambridge: Cambridge University Press.

Vaizey, J. (1972) *The Political Economy of Education*. London: Duckworth.

Webster, C. (1998) *The National Health Service: A political history*. Oxford: Oxford University Press.

West, E.G. (1970) 'Resource allocation and growth in early nineteenth-century education'. *Economic History Review*, 24(4), 633–42.

— (1975) 'Educational slowdown and public intervention in nineteenth-century England: a study in the economics of bureaucracy'. *Explorations in Economic History*, 12, 61–87.

Wiener, M.J. (1981) *English Culture and the Decline of the Industrial Spirit 1850–1980*. Cambridge: Cambridge University Press.

3 'The Member for Education': the life and times of the University of London's final Member of Parliament, Sir Ernest Graham-Little (1867–1950)

David Crook

Introduction

Richard Aldrich's intimate knowledge of the Institute of Education (Aldrich 2002) and of the federal University of London has, for many years, delighted and interested his students and colleagues. The future of the University of London and its impressive Senate House head-quarters is difficult to predict following the recent secession of Imperial College and the granting of degree-awarding powers to several institutions, but the developing partnerships between the Institute and other medium-sized colleges of the University mark a new chapter in the history of academic life in Bloomsbury, the origins of which are discussed in this chapter.

As a distinguished dermatologist, Sir Ernest Graham-Little's stand-ing remains high more than 50 years after his death (Monk 2003, 2005), but as a politician – he was the last Member of Parliament (MP) for the University of London – and personality, he remains largely unknown. His wife, Lady Helen, who lived until 1968, twice referred to a memoir of her husband that she was preparing, mentioning also that family papers might one day be deposited in the British Museum (*The Times*, 4 May 1955: 15; 16 July 1956: 15). Neither intention was accomplished, but other evidence, most notably from *The Times*, has made it possible to piece together a biographical story of a fascinating character.

Family life and medical career

Born on 8 February 1867, Ernest Gordon Graham Little was the only child of Michael Little, an Indian Civil Servant and his wife, Anna, daughter of Alexander English from Cape Town. At the age of 4, when his mother died, Ernest travelled to South Africa where his uncle, Frederick Alexander English, became his guardian. He was to receive an elite education at the South African College, the forerunner of the University of Cape Town, from 1882 to 1887, where he headed the honours list in literature and philosophy and graduated with a BA in 1887. As a recipient of a Porter Scholarship he travelled to study medicine briefly in Paris and then at Guy's and St George's hospitals, University of London.

Graham-Little's public recollections of his early life were infrequent and selective. He remembered his 'deep depression' as an overseas student, 'pitchforked, at the age of 20, from South Africa into the gloom of "The Borough"' (ibid., 8 June 1925, letter: 10) and that he had been 'a shy and awkward youth, dropped from a tiny South African township into this monstrous city where I had no relatives and no friends' (Graham Little 1926: 1). His claim (Morris-Jones 1959; rev. Berridge 2004) to have sustained his medical training by scholarships and prizes seems improbable, given that his guardian was a claim-holder to the De Beers Kimberley mine and a business associate of Cecil Rhodes (Williams 1921: 46–7). The fortune that English amassed from diamond mining enabled him, in 1898, to purchase Addington Palace, the stone-built Georgian summer residence of archbishops of Canterbury, set in an estate of some 1,200 acres. Over the next decade,

English spent over £100,000 on the building, which was remodelled by Richard Norman Shaw, the leading architect of his day (*The Times*, 4 September 1928: 15).

As Ernest Little entered his thirties, his confidence had grown. In 1899, while working as an assistant physician at the East London Hospital for Children in Shadwell, he ventured beyond his specialism of mainstream dermatology to deliver a controversial address (as Ernest Graham Little) on 'The causation of night terrors' to the British Medical Association (BMA) (Graham Little 1899). Materially, as well as mentally, he was more comfortable now, being settled in the exclusive medical quarter of London. At the time of the 1901 census he was living at 61 Wimpole Street with another uncle, Arthur, and three female servants. One year later, he became Consulting Physician to the Skin Department at St Mary's, the leading teaching hospital of the University of London and a 'recognised teacher' of internal students. He continued to work at St Mary's until retiring from medicine in 1934.

In 1906 Graham Little joined the University's External Council and Senate and, 23 years later, he became a founder member of the University Court. Committee work brought him into contact with his future wife, the daughter of an American shipping agent, a resident of fashionable Chester Terrace, a graduate of Queen Mary College and organiser-secretary of the University of London Graduates' Association (ULGA). The early life of Sara Helen Kauffmann-Kendall, whose marriage to Graham Little was announced in *The Times* (24 October 1911: 1), presents a fascinating study in social mobility. The 1881 census identifies her as Nelly Kendall, the eldest of three children born in Chelsea to Prussian émigrés. Following her marriage, however, the name Sara was discarded in favour of Helen, just as Nelly had been abandoned earlier. There was to be one further name change for both spouses: in 1931, to accompany his knighthood, Sir Ernest and Lady Helen adopted their double-barrelled surname (ibid., 25 February 1931: 17).

Graham-Little's specialist field of dermatology was transformed by medical procedures developed during the First World War, when he served as Consulting Dermatologist to London's military hospitals. Remarkably, his own prominence in the field came after his election to Parliament in 1924, when he worked mornings at St Mary's and divided the remainder of his time between the House of Commons, University committees and functions and private consulting from Wimpole Street. His medical writings included many contributions to *The Lancet* and the *British Medical Journal*, as well as specialist dermatological journals. As a scalp expert, he diagnosed Graham Little-Piccardi-Lasseur syndrome, endorsed certain hair products in newspaper advertisements and condemned others in court as an expert witness. He was a consultant to such organisations as the Concert Artistes' Association and the National Union of Teachers (NUT), led British delegations to international conferences and accepted honorary appointments in at least eight countries. Graham-Little completed terms as president of the British Association of Dermatologists and the Dermatological Sections of the Royal Society of Medicine and BMA, though he regularly found himself in disagreement with the latter organisation's flirtation with the 'Socialist' idea of a universal state medical service (ibid., 11 October 1930: 14). His vision for medicine was founded upon supporting and expanding voluntary hospitals such as St Mary's independently of the State. Following publication of the 1942 Beveridge Report, he heavily attacked the BMA for supporting 'the most menacing challenge to all the concepts of life for which society stood, and to the maintenance of our freedom and liberty' (ibid., 3 December 1942, letter: 5; 8 October 1943: 7). Throughout 1946 he resisted the National Health Service (NHS) Bill in Parliament and later encouraged trainee doctors and dentists to escape the 'totalitarian control' of the Bevan Act by emigrating to the Dominions (ibid., 24 October 1947, letter: 5). In a final act of defiance before leaving Westminster, he confounded Ministry of Health officials by demanding information relating to costs for providing sight testing and spectacles in the opening months of the NHS (ibid., 30 October 1948: 3). This was entirely in character: back in 1926 he had advised the secretary of the Medical Research

Council that 'Government departments are there to be shot at' (letter, 20 November 1946, FD1/1979, National Archives [NA]).

Following their 1911 marriage, the Graham Littles moved to a larger Wimpole Street property, number 40. Helen bore a son, Esmond, and a daughter, Helen junior, and, by the early 1920s, she had taken her place in London society as a well-known hostess of charity dances and other fund-raising events for London's voluntary hospitals. From 1931 the family featured regularly in the 'Court Circular' and 'Invalids' columns of *The Times*, announcing their holiday departures, destinations and return dates, illnesses, accidents and recoveries. The presentation of Helen junior as a general circle debutante at the first court of the social 'season' was also recorded (*The Times*, 21 May 1931: 20). Like her parents, she was also a serial name-changer: it was as 'Violet' Graham-Little that she played Helena from *All's Well That Ends Well* in a 1932 pageant to raise funds for the People's League of Health at Grosvenor House, but as 'Helen Viola' that she organised a cabaret at Claridge's in her capacity as vice-chairman of the Young People's Committee of the National Council for Maternity and Child Welfare (ibid., 24 February 1932: 10; 13 May 1932: 17). In July of that year, following the last in a series of Monday afternoon tea dances at 40 Wimpole Street and the beginning of the parliamentary recess, it was reported that the family would be leaving London (ibid., 11 July 1932: 15). The summer was to end in tragedy when Helen junior, aged 19, was drowned whilst bathing at Saltdean (ibid., 3 September: 12; 5 September: 7). Her brother's efforts to save her life were later marked by an award from the Humane Society (ibid., 28 December 1932: 13).

Ernest was admitted to the Folk-Lore Society at the end of 1932, chairing discussion of a paper entitled 'Whence comes the fear of ghosts and evil spirits' early the next year (*Folk-Lore: Transactions of the Folk-Lore Society* XLIV(1): 2), but the Graham-Littles temporarily withdrew from the London social scene, returning in 1934 to host a week of parties in their box at the Royal Albert Hall during the *Pageant of Parliament* (*The Times*, 23 July 1934: 17). In the words of Bob Boothby, for the most-advantaged social group the unemployed were 'out of sight and out of mind' during the 1930s (1978: 67), but in the admittedly comfortable surroundings of the Dorchester Hotel and Claridge's Lady Helen hosted 'Good Companions' fund-raising events for the unemployed (*The Times*, 7 October 1936: 15; 3 November 1936: 19), a ball for the Waifs and Strays Society and a bridge tournament for the Boys' Hostels Association (ibid., 16 December 1936: 17; 21 January 1938: 17).

Ernest and Helen maintained a close-knit circle of friends, mostly associated with the University and many from the medical quarter. As war approached, one friendship beyond these constituencies had to be sacrificed: Herbert von Dirksen, former ambassador to the Court of St James, was described in an obituary note by Lady Helen as 'an honourable representative of a dishonourable regime' and the antithesis of his predecessor, von Ribbentrop (ibid., 31 December 1955: 9). War profoundly affected the Graham-Littles in three ways. First, it led to Ernest's temporary return, at the age of 73, to the Skin Department of St Mary's Hospital. Second, in 1941 their home, 40 Wimpole Street, which housed a collection of priceless Japanese art, was entirely destroyed by Luftwaffe bombing ('Obituary: Sir Ernest Graham-Little, M.D., F.R.C.P.', *British Medical Journal*, 4684, 14 October 1950: 894–5). Finally, ten years after their daughter's death, Esmond also perished on active service with the Royal Air Force Volunteer Reserve, aged 27 (*The Times*, 16 June 1942: 1).

The politics of the University of London

First elected in 1906 to represent the powerful constituency of Medicine, Graham-Little's membership of the University of London Senate was to continue until 1950. During these 44 years he was re-elected no fewer than ten times, with strong backing from the ULGA. Still more significant, however, was his unbroken membership of the University's External Council, also from 1906. Since being chartered, in 1836, provision for University of London external students (those studying at home or overseas for degrees without being attached to a particular college or school) had helped to secure London's unique position as the imperial university.

Distinct Academic and External Councils were established after the 1898 University of London Act and, from his earliest association with the University, Graham-Little was a supporter of the 'external side'. He rejected the regularly stated views that this work stymied London's development as a modern university, that it divided the memberships of Senate and other committees and that it was incompatible with the day-to-day teaching work of its colleges. In 1913 a Royal Commission, under the chairmanship of Lord Haldane, called for the abolition of the External Council and the establishment of a new administrative centre to replace its headquarters in the Imperial Institute, South Kensington. A site in Bloomsbury, north of the British Museum, was thought to be the most appropriate location for the University's nucleus and a departmental committee was quickly formed to consider how the report could be put into effect. Graham Little was one of five members of an External Council deputation that defended the status quo (ibid., 30 March 1914: 4).

With the outbreak of war, this departmental committee was disbanded, but the question of relocating the University's base re-emerged in 1920 when H.A.L. Fisher, president of the Board of Education, offered an 11.5-acre site in Bloomsbury, which had been purchased from the Duke of Bedford for £425,000. What followed was to prove embarrassing for the University, because the land purchase presupposed that the authorities of King's College would be willing to surrender its Crown-leased buildings in the Strand, which they were not. Meanwhile, on the assumption that King's would transfer, a range of smaller University institutions, including the Institute of Historical Research (IHR), founded by A.F. Pollard of University College, began to occupy buildings on the site. A London University Defence Committee was formed and Graham Little attacked Pollard for being 'too impressed with the advantages of the Bloomsbury site, so conveniently near University College'. It was, he believed, an 'unnecessary project at a time when, for example, our great voluntary hospitals –

and many other equally urgently needed institutions – are threatened with extinction for lack of funds' (ibid., 12 May 1922, letter: 8). Further opposition to the Bloomsbury plan was forthcoming from the ULGA, of which Graham Little became president in 1923. Knowing that it had been stipulated that if the Bloomsbury site was not in use by April 1926 the land would be sold back to the Duke of Bedford (Harte 1986: 203), the UGLA sought to focus efforts on acquiring further University space in South Kensington.

Already well immersed in the politics of the University, a sequence of events during the summer of 1924 was to change the life of Dr Ernest Graham Little, propelling him into the arena of Westminster politics. On 14 July the University's Unionist MP, also a distinguished physician, Sir Sydney Russell-Wells, suffered a fatal seizure (*The Times*, 15 July 1924: 14). For many years Wells had strongly supported the ULGA and the external examinations side. Two years earlier he had seen off challenges for the seat from A.F. Pollard, the Liberal candidate, and also H.G. Wells for the Labour Party. The possibility of a contentious by-election became a certainty when, in August, the Labour president of the Board of Education, Sir Charles Trevelyan, announced the establishment of another departmental committee to examine the recommendations of the Haldane Report. This was to be chaired by Lord Ernle, with a membership that included Sir Lewis Selby-Bigge, the Board's permanent secretary, Sir Robert Blair, the outgoing education officer for the London County Council (LCC) and Graham Little's nemesis, A.F. Pollard.

Pollard was again adopted as the Liberal candidate, notwithstanding his membership of the Ernle Committee, while the Conservative Party put forward another known supporter of the Bloomsbury project, Sir John Rose Bradford of University College, who, like Pollard, had served on the post-Haldane departmental committee. Suspicions that Pollard and Bradford were tainted by their pasts caused the non-political ULGA to conclude that there should be a candidate standing on an anti-Haldane ticket. One person, above all, seemed ideally suited: the ULGA president, Dr Ernest Graham Little.

Graham Little's candidature, announced in a letter to *The Times* on 19 August 1924, presented the forthcoming by-election as an opportunity to save external degrees and, indeed, to wrest the University of London from the clutches of University College. He quoted Pollard's hope, as expressed to the Haldane Committee more than a decade earlier, to see 'the abolition of the granting of a degree without any teaching' and cast doubt upon Bradford's conversion to acceptance of the external side (ibid., 19 August 1924, letter: 6). Subsequently, his election address stated that 'an attempt is now in preparation to destroy the University as we know it' and 'if you now return a candidate who has throughout opposed the Haldane recommendations, they will be killed once and for all'. He pledged to

> fight for freedom of the University from bureaucratic control, government of the University by its graduates and teachers, maintenance of external degrees, preservation of the present relations between secondary schools and the University, and the free and harmonious development of both sides of the University – the conservation of the standard of its degrees and of the central control of the University of degree examinations.
>
> (ibid., 25 August 1924: 7)

A central plank of his first election campaign was an appeal to London graduates with an interest in promoting state education, including those working as schoolteachers. If elected, he declared, 'I shall regard myself as "Member for Education", not debarred from speaking and voting on other subjects, but holding a special brief for those engaged in educational work'. 'No boy or girl of real capacity to profit from secondary education should be debarred by poverty from attending it', he maintained, while on the subject of teachers' pay and pensions, it was his view that:

> Teachers (graduates from our University and others) have been disgracefully underpaid in the past. . . . Their salary should be adequate to provide a reasonable competence and to place the profession of teaching in fair competition with other professions and callings, so as

to attract to it the best entrants. In the interests of the State I would support the provision of pensions for teachers, both in aided and unaided schools, if those schools are efficiently conducted.

This manifesto was independent in every sense, one that persuaded Sir James Yoxall, former general secretary of the NUT, to write in support of Graham Little in preference to Pollard, the candidate for the Liberal Party that he had himself served as an MP for 24 years (ibid., 4 October 1924: 12).

Labour Prime Minister James Ramsay MacDonald's decision to call a general election at the end of October 1924 meant that the London University poll was no longer to be a by-election. Graham Little, standing as an Independent, emerged victorious from the contest, securing a narrow majority of 389 over Bradford, his closest rival. Immediately, the new MP called upon the new Conservative prime minister, Stanley Baldwin, and president of the Board of Education, Lord Eustace Percy, to discharge the Trevelyan Committee. There was no need for an inquiry, Graham Little wrote: the University was successful and neither its Senate nor Convocation had been consulted by the Board of Education about the purposes or personnel of the committee. He remained concerned that the committee's membership included Pollard, 'the most active protagonist in favour of the Haldane recommendation, which advised the concentration of the two incorporated colleges, University College and King's College, and of the University headquarters upon the Bloomsbury site'. King's College, by contrast, was unrepresented on the Committee (ibid., 29 November 1924, letter: 8).

Percy proceeded with the inquiry, and despite assurances that the value of the external side was now better understood (Dunsheath and Miller 1958: 122), Ernle's resignation as chairman, in February 1925, on health grounds, and replacement by E. Hilton Young, introduced a new element of uncertainty. Moreover, Graham Little continued to maintain that Bloomsbury was 'an increasingly undesirable' location for the University headquarters, with hotels, businesses and flats limiting the possibilities for student housing (*The Times*, 8 June 1925, letter: 10). This argument incensed Pollard, not only because the IHR, as well as the University of London Union and an architecture studio were now established on the Bloomsbury campus, but also because Graham Little had publicly referred to confidential Senate documents (ibid., 12 June 1925, letter: 12). The Hilton Young Report was published in March 1926. It identified 'a growing sense of harmony' between the internal and external sides (Board of Education 1926: 9), as represented by the Academic and External Councils, and supported external degrees. But it also provided ammunition for the government to proceed with a Parliamentary Bill, designed to centralise the University, to re-constitute its Senate and to recognise its various institutions as 'schools' in one or more faculties. For Graham Little, this amounted to unwarranted interference. In the Commons, he led the opposition and, outside it, he organised like-minded speakers to lobby MPs to vote against the Bill. He also accepted the nomination of Senate, in June 1926, against a backdrop of the General Strike, to contest the election for vice-chancellor, only to be defeated by a narrow 26–21 vote by Sir William Beveridge, director of the London School of Economics (LSE) since 1919 (Beveridge 1953: 192–3).

The contest was a bitter one, with Beveridge accusing Graham Little of buying support with free dinners (Harris 1977: 270) and the two-year period of his vice-chancellorship, during which the Bill passed into law, witnessed their mutual dislike intensify. Beveridge reluctantly conceded that 'The University of London . . . has and will, no doubt, always have its characteristic and valuable external side', but he affirmed that it 'is now, like other universities, mainly a teaching university' (*The Times*, 24 July 1926, letter: 8). The enactment of the Bill, at the end of 1926, represented a further defeat for Graham Little: commissioners, whose number included Percy Nunn, principal and professor of the London Day Training College (later the Institute of Education), were appointed to make new statutes 'in general accordance with the recommendations contained in the report of the [Hilton Young] Committee' (quoted in Harte 1986: 213). Eventually implemented in 1929, the statutes revised the composition of Senate and a new executive body, the Court, was established. A third defeat for Graham Little followed in February 1927, when Senate voted narrowly to accept a gift of £400,000 from the New York-based Rockefeller Foundation, at last securing the purchase of the Bloomsbury site.

The prospect of better relations with the vice-chancellor seemed distant in 1928 when Sir Gregory Foster, principal of University College, who had opposed Graham Little's candidature in 1924, succeeded Beveridge. But Foster's acknowledgement of the doubling of external work in less than 30 years, together with the fact that Graham Little's friend, A.N. Whitehead, the philosopher and mathematician of Imperial College, now chaired the Academic Council, eased tensions (*The Times*, 9 May 1929: 13). Gregory's successor as vice-chancellor, Rev. John Scott Lidgett, was another personal friend. He secured additional funding for the establishment of central buildings, and sites for Birkbeck College and the London Day Training College totalling £450,000 from the LCC, on which he had served for many years in various capacities, as well as £50,000 from the Goldsmiths' Company for the University Library (ibid., 30 November 1931: 17). A further Rockefeller grant permitted the London School of Hygiene and Tropical Medicine, of which Graham Little was a governor, to take its place as a school of the University and, in June 1933, King George V laid the foundation stone for Senate House, the centrepiece of architect Charles Holden's plans for the University in Bloomsbury. In the following year, one speaker enthused about 'the most ambitious individual building programme since the time of Wren', of the 12 medical schools comprising the medical faculty and of further bene-factions from the City of London and private individuals. The speaker in question was none other than Sir Ernest Graham-Little, formerly the fiercest opponent of the project (ibid., 12 October 1934: 19). The first phase of the plans, which were only ever partially realised, opened, on schedule, in August 1936.

Parliamentary elections

The university franchise may be dated back to 1603 for Oxford and Cambridge universities and, in London's case, to 1868. The first University of London MP had been Robert Lowe, former vice-president of the Committee of Council on Education and originator of 'payment by results'. Lowe (1868–80) and his successor Sir John Lubbock (1880–1900) were both Liberals, but the next three MPs for the seat, Sir Michael Foster (1900–6), Sir Philip Magnus (1906–22) and Sir Sydney Russell-Wells (1922–4) were Unionists.

At one level, the university constituencies were the last remaining 'rotten boroughs', permitting a select few a second vote. In the instance of London, this was secured by a payment to become a life member of Convocation. When an election was called, eligible voters were sent ballot papers by mail, irrespective of their location in the world. Upon expressing their preference for a candidate and having their own signature witnessed, the papers were sent to the vice-chancellor, who served as the returning officer. In contrast to orthodox constituencies, the state of the votes cast was publicly declared each evening until the ballot closed (Rex 1946: 203–4). Following his narrow electoral majority in 1924, Ernest Graham Little was to be re-elected to Parliament at four subsequent general elections, in 1929, 1931, 1935 and 1945.

In the 1924 campaign, the influential former MP, Sir Philip Magnus, supported Bradford, the Conservative candidate. Subsequently, however, Magnus took the view that Graham Little should not be opposed by a London University Conservative and Unionist Association candidate and that, if possible, he should rejoin the Association from which he had resigned in 1924. Graham Little confirmed in his second campaign address that he was a 'Conservative of life-long conviction', but staunch association members were neither prepared to forgive his earlier disloyalty nor his opposition to the University of London Bill, promoted by a Conservative government. In the event, Sir John Gilbert, the Conservative candidate in 1929 finished a poor third behind Graham Little and the Liberal Walter Layton, editor of *The Economist* (*The Times*, 12 November 1928: 13; 14 November 1928: 13; 16 November 1928: 18).

Graham Little was a political outsider by choice. There were occasions when he joined forces with his fellow MPs: he served terms as chair of the Parliamentary Medical Committee and the Committee of University Members of the House of Commons, but he believed that too many medical parliamentarians lobbied slavishly for medical organisations and that the imperial position of London made it unlike any other British university (Cooter 2004; *The Times*, 10 December 1943: 4; 18 February 1944: 2). Isolation had its advantages: addressing a 1930 luncheon of the Society of Individualists, of which he was a member, he took as his theme 'The blessed privilege of being independent' (ibid., 14 May 1930: 19).

Against a backdrop of economic crisis in June 1931, Ramsay MacDonald's second Labour administration was defeated in the Commons by just four votes on a proposal to abolish the university franchises. The subsequent creation of a national government, to which the recently knighted Graham-Little showed loyalty through his voting record, may have provided good reason to expect that he would be returned, unopposed, in the October general election. The Conservative and Liberal associations decided not to field candidates and, for Labour, Ramsay MacDonald's stated principle was that the party in possession should claim the national candidature. Shortly before nominations closed, however, Major Archibald Church declared his intention to stand, also as an Independent, having failed to secure party support to continue as Labour MP for another London constituency (Bassett 1958: 296). The electorate was, however, swayed by arguments that this was an unnecessary contest at a time of national crisis. Graham-Little took a 73 per cent share of the vote, increasing his majority by more than 2,300.

In 1935 the University's Conservative and Unionist Association again opted to support Graham-Little as the national government candidate, but he declined to stand as a Conservative (*The Times*, 1 March 1935: 6;

2 November 1935: 7). This time, his share of the vote fell only marginally and he comprehensively defeated his single opponent, Labour's Sir Norman Angell, the pacifist author, lecturer and Nobel Prize winner. Having voted to abolish the university constituencies four years earlier, Angell's credibility had been in doubt. An unsatisfactory feature of the university franchise became evident during this contest: Graham-Little's election agent, Rev. Dr H.B. Workman, happened also to be the deputy vice-chancellor and the person who, in the event of the vice-chancellor becoming incapacitated, would act as returning officer (ibid., 2 November 1935: 7). More personal suggestions of impropriety were to follow in February 1937, in a scurrilous *University of London Union Magazine* article. This hinted that Graham-Little exerted undue influence over University appointments and promotions, favouring those who voted for him. Just as an amicable settlement appeared to be in sight, parts of the article were re-published in *The Spectator*. Graham-Little pursued a successful libel case against both publications (file VP 1/12, University of London archives; *The Times*, 3 May 1938: 5; 4 May 1938: 4).

There was to be one further parliamentary contest, in 1945, when Graham-Little narrowly defeated Mary Stocks, principal of Westfield College, by 149 votes following a recount, though it should be acknowledged that the electoral roll had been significantly reduced by difficulties in finding addresses for overseas-based constituents. Stocks had been persuaded to stand as an 'Independent Progressive' by a committee headed by Beveridge. The campaign was notable for 'a lively exchange of printed announcements' between the candidates (ibid., 13 March 1945: 2; Rex 1946: 210).

Attlee's landslide victory meant that Labour was, after 1945, in a position to do what it had failed to achieve in 1929–31: abolish the university franchise. The 1948 Representation of the People Act swept away the 12 seats representing seven universities and only four of the sitting MPs sought re-election elsewhere. Coinciding with his retirement from the University of London Senate after ten successive re-elections, Graham-Little left the House of Commons, aged 83, in

February 1950. He journeyed to Wimpole Lodge, his country home in Epsom, named after the London street where he had resided for almost half a century. It was here that he died eight months later.

Education and other interests

Always a more articulate writer than orator, Graham-Little contributed articles and correspondence on a vast array of topics to periodicals which included the *Edinburgh Review*, *Empire Review*, the *Journal of Negro History*, the *Nineteenth Century* and *Notes and Queries*, as well as dermatology and general medical journals and the press. Taken overall, his public outputs reflect his passions and prejudices: he was strongly for high standards of medical practice and professionalism, medical education for women, imperialism, individualism, and the voluntary hospitals, and no less strongly against socialism, unwarranted State interference and superfluous spending. But they reveal another, contradictory, side to the man, too. Although he denounced medical quackery, which in his career had seen the 'essentials' of surgery and midwifery undermined by the 'cults' of osteopaths, chiropractitioners, medical herbalists and Christian scientists (*The Times*, 19 October 1933: 5), he was himself a devotee of pseudo-scientific eugenicism. In a 1931 public lecture he stated that the 'social problem class' had 'brought into practical politics as a serious and indeed necessary proposition the practice of sterilisation of the unfit, either as a voluntary or as a compulsory measure' (ibid., 24 February 1931: 7). Other interventions saw him offer 'scientific' explanations for the 'mental backwardness' and 'early senility' of native Africans (ibid., 28 August 1934: 6).

General health issues were always of interest to Graham-Little. His maiden Commons speech supported the Summer Time Bill on the grounds that hospitals could turn 'a wreck of humanity' into a 'reasonably healthy person' by sitting a patient in front of a carbon arc lamp for 30 minutes three times a week (Hansard, HC (series 5) vol. 179, cols. 1761–2, 13 March 1925). During the Second World War he condemned the Ministry of Food's 'national loaf', comprising white bread, fortified with calcium and vitamin B1, and he played a part in triggering the resignation of Bob Boothby, parliamentary secretary to the Ministry of Food, whose company, Roche Products, had a financial interest supplying the vitamin additives. The failure to endorse wholemeal bread, Graham-Little argued, 'constitutes a retrograde policy which may prove disastrous to the nation's security', not least because too many young women existed on a midday meal of 'tea and buns', the latter made from white flour of negligible nutritive value (*The Times*, 17 December 1940: 2; 7 October 1941: 5). In the final years of his life, as an expert on venereal disease, he supported Marie Stopes and corresponded at length with Geoffrey Fisher, archbishop of Canterbury, and others over the question of contraceptive slot machines (Machin 1998: 153–4).

Graham-Little championed the playing of chess and the interests of both the motorist and the pedestrian, sometimes combining these passions by driving to European chess congresses. He established a chess circle at the Athenaeum Club and, after his 1924 general election victory, became honorary secretary of the House of Commons' circle (*The Times*, 11 March 1926: 19). It was on a two-month continental motoring holiday, he claimed in his 1935 election address, that he came to a better understanding of other nations' envy of Britain's economic stability and political freedom (ibid., 31 October 1935: 9). But a rare exception to Graham-Little's abhorrence of State interference with individual freedom was manifested in his support for a vehicle speed limit for built-up areas, and as joint chairman of the Road Accidents Parliamentary Group he demanded a more searching test than the 1934 Road Traffic Act's specification of 'competence to drive' (ibid., 23 April 1934, letter: 10).

What of Graham-Little's 1924 promise to serve as 'Member for Education'? At that point in his life he was convinced that the Board of Education was trying to control universities in the same way that it controlled primary and much secondary education: 'Lord Haldane was obviously completely in love with the German system of State-controlled universities, and his Commission reflected that feeling very faithfully', he told a 1926 audience (ibid., 13 November 1926: 14).

Throughout his parliamentary career he maintained an interest in teachers' pay, advising in 1930 that 'The elementary school teacher begins at a salary of £160 a year, that is, two-thirds of the wages that are paid to the street cleaners in the district in which I live' (Hansard, HC (series 5) vol. 239, col. 1612, 29 May 1930). His interests in schooling were mostly confined to its relationship with children's health. He pressed for children to be given pasteurised, rather than untreated, milk in schools (*The Times*, 30 April 1934, letter: 19; 8 May 1934, letter: 12), considered expectations that children should complete homework at night to be an 'outrage' and damaging to their mental health (*British Paramount News*, 27 February 1936, BGX407212066, ITN archive), and was a founder member of a campaign to 'Abolish "slum" schools' (*The Times*, 30 January 1937: 7). In 1938 he became drawn into lengthy correspondence with Cyril Norwood, chairman of the Secondary Schools Examinations Council, about the decision to separate the School Certificate Examination from university matriculation. Graham-Little was accused of failing to understand 'that it is the business of school examinations to follow school curricula', and of being unable to see beyond the interests of the external side of London University and the 'diminishing splendour of the "London Matric"' (ibid., 5 December 1938, letter by Norwood: 8; 17 January 1939, letter by J.C. Dent, Westminster City School: 8). On the 1944 Education Act, Graham-Little was, predictably, unenthusiastic, calling it an 'instrument of social equality' (*Daily Sketch*, 15 March 1946, letter). In the period following the Act he pursued Ellen Wilkinson and George Tomlinson, Attlee's Education ministers and their civil servants about the country's readiness to implement the raising of the school-leaving age to 15, and was a strong critic of the one-year emergency training scheme for teachers, arguing that such a programme would not be tolerated by other professions (Crook 1997: 384–5). But some interventions demonstrated misunderstandings of state education: in 1942, a note by a civil servant contemplated 'a temptation to pull the hon. Member's tail' when writing to return correspondence on the grounds that 'So many of his questions are based on no grounds!' (note by 'EHS', 22 October 1942, ED 34/116, NA).

In regard to University of London matters he was typically better informed, but in his opposition to the Hilton Young Report and University of London Bill in the mid-1920s he felt thwarted by Oxbridge MPs' identification of London as 'the poor man's university' (Hansard, HC (series 5) vol. 199, col. 2127, 19 November 1926). He spoke up for London students, objecting, for example, to the temporary closure of the Botanic Gardens to save money and he pressed for extended opening hours for the British Museum Reading Room (*The Times*, 17 June 1931, letter: 15; 8 September 1937, letter: 8). Even in wartime he challenged plans to station members of the Auxiliary Territorial Service at Royal Holloway College, and for the Ministry of Information to take over the School of Oriental and African Studies (ibid., 9 June 1941, letter: 5; 21 December 1942, letter: 2).

Conclusion

The concept of the university franchise seems anachronistic today, yet it is interesting that Churchill promised to restore these constituencies after 1951 and, as recently as 1982, a Conservative backbencher sought unsuccessfully to introduce a private member's Bill for their revival (ibid., 1 December 1982: 1). Graham-Little's most significant, though unintentional, contribution to the Commons was to establish a trend, from the 1930s, for university candidates to stand as Independents. Much more recently, the election, in 2001, of Dr Richard Taylor marked the return of the Independent medical MP to Westminster.

The University of London's external work and schools of medicine were the sources of Graham-Little's greatest pride and interest in education. He was always better disposed towards some colleges than others: Birkbeck was too closely associated with Haldane, University College with Pollard and the LSE with Beveridge. In 1934 Beveridge came close to instigating a libel suit after Graham-Little had termed the LSE 'a hotbed of Communist teaching' (Kramnick and Sheerman 1993: 329–30) and, four years later, he branded the MP 'incorrigible' for having apparently erased from his memory his original opposition to the Rockefeller grant (*The Times*, 21 November 1935: 10). The men were to cross swords again during the 1940s over the Beveridge Report and during the 1945 parliamentary contest.

This portrait of Ernest Graham-Little's life and career in academic and national politics has revealed him to be an intriguing man, whose privileged life was also touched by great sadness. He was a brilliant dermatologist, but as a man he could be provocative and pompous. Some of the views he held would now be regarded as unacceptable and underpinned by flawed science. Only to a limited extent did Graham-Little fulfil his promise to serve as the 'Member for Education'.

References

Aldrich, R. (2002) *The Institute of Education 1902–2002. A centenary history*. London: Institute of Education.

Bassett, R. (1958) *Nineteen Thirty-one: Political crisis*. London: Macmillan.

Beveridge, Lord (1953) *Power and Influence*. New York: Beechhurst Press.

Board of Education (1926) *Report of the Departmental Committee on the University of London* (Hilton Young Report). London: HMSO.

Boothby, R. (1978) *Boothby: Recollections of a rebel*. London: Hutchinson.

Cooter, R. (2004) 'The rise and decline of the medical member: doctors and Parliament in Edwardian and interwar Britain'. *Bulletin of the History of Medicine*, 78(1), 59–107.

Crook, D. (1997) 'Challenge, response and dilution: a revisionist view of the Emergency Training Scheme for Teachers, 1945–1951'. *Cambridge Journal of Education*, 27(3), 379–89.

Dunsheath, P. and Miller, M. (1958) *Convocation in the University of London: The first hundred years*. London: Athlone Press.

Graham Little, E. (1899) 'The causation of night terrors'. *British Medical Journal*, 2016, 19 August, 464–5.

— (1926) 'Doctors and the public: an address delivered at the opening of the medical session at St. George's Medical School'. Privately printed.

Harris, J. (1977) *William Beveridge: A biography*. Oxford: Clarendon Press.

Harte, N. (1986) *The University of London 1836–1986: An illustrated history*. London: Athlone Press.

Kramnick, I. and Sheerman, B. (1993) *Harold Laski: A life on the Left*. London: Hamish Hamilton.

Machin, G.I.T. (1998) *Churches and Social Issues in Twentieth-century Britain*. Oxford: Clarendon Press.

Monk, B.E. (2003) 'Sir Ernest Graham-Little, dermatologist and politician'. *British Journal of Dermatology*, 149 (Suppl. 64), 57.

— (2005) 'Sir Ernest Graham-Little, MP, MD, FRCP (1867–1950): dermatologist and politician'. *Journal of Medical Biography*, 13(2), 89–94.

Morris-Jones, H. (1959) 'Little, Sir Ernest Gordon Graham Graham- (1867–1950)', rev. V. Berridge (2004). In *Oxford Dictionary of National Biography*. Oxford: Oxford University Press.

Rex, M.B. (1946) 'The university constituencies in the recent British election'. *Journal of Politics*, 8(2), 201–11.

Williams, B. (1921) *Cecil Rhodes*. New York: Henry Holt and Company.

4 Gender and policy in Birmingham, 1902–44

Ruth Watts

Introduction

Some of the research in this chapter was part of my work on women in science, supported and thoughtfully critiqued by Richard Aldrich. I cannot thank him enough for his encouragement of many years and I know I am just one among many. As an ex-president of the UK History of Education Society and former executive member of the International Standing Conference for the History of Education, I should also like to thank Richard for his creative and scholarly leadership in both. In particular, he made such a vital contribution to keeping the History of Education Society going at a time when it could have been destroyed by the withdrawal of the subject from initial teacher training.

In the late nineteenth century, Birmingham was a leader in educational and civic progress, its school board and city council alike dominated by a liberal elite in which Quakers and Unitarians played a prominent role. Between 1902 and 1944, the City of Birmingham Local Education Authority (Birmingham LEA), heir to the Birmingham School Board, sought to implement the changing educational policies and ideas emanating from national government in a city which grew to be the second largest in England. This chapter will examine the work done by women of the Birmingham LEA, identify who they were, which committees they served on and any significant contribution they made. It will also discuss whether educational policies towards males and females were differentiated, using the example of the teaching of science and mathematics.

In recent years, various studies have explored the role of women in education in local government (e.g. Hollis 1989; Martin 1999; Goodman and Harrop 2000). In doing so, they have uncovered both aspects of education and government previously largely ignored and important opportunities taken by women which transgressed the public–private divide. At the same time, it has been shown that such women often reinforced class and gender notions through the maternalist roles they assumed.

Local government and women, 1902–44

By 1900, elected borough councils in the urban areas and county, parish and rural councils in the rural areas, had taken over much of the tangled web of local administration. But education was administered by separate locally elected school boards. After the 1902 Education Act, these school boards were replaced by new local education authorities (LEAs); that is, education committees of the elected councils. These had responsibility for all elementary education to 14 and statutory rights to establish secondary schooling, seen as a more academic education and mainly for a different social class (Jenkins and Swinnerton 1998: viii). In Birmingham, the LEA converted old higher grade schools and subsequently had two fee-paying secondary schools with departments for boys and girls, and one for boys only. It also had a municipal technical school. When the boundaries of Birmingham were enlarged in 1911, more secondary schools were built and extra places were added in the 1920s. In response to the Hadow Report of 1926, the LEA developed further the upper classes in elementary schools and built senior elementary schools so that there was separate provision for over-11s. It continued to fund or aid a small but growing number of secondary grammar schools, some single sex and others with boys' and girls' departments. From 1923, admission to all these secondary schools and others aided by the council, with the exception of the two King Edward VI high schools, was by entrance exam (City of Birmingham Education Committee [CBEC] *Reports* 1903: 11–12; 1911: 10; 1930: 96–101, University of Birmingham Special Collections [UBSC]). LEAs had quite considerable powers, yet were bound by the regulations of Acts of Parliament and the Board of Education (Eyken 1973; Hunt 1991: 8–13, 19–21).

Although until 1918 all women and some men did not have the parliamentary vote, since 1872 unmarried women ratepayers had the borough vote (Hollis 1989: 2–3, 7–8). Women ratepayers could also vote for, and stand for, election to the school boards: a number did so and made a 'positive contribution' to the formation of state education and social welfare (Martin 1999: 147). When, however, the school boards were abolished and education put under the remit of the local borough and county councils in 1902, women could serve only as co-opted members and, therefore, would be unable to see their proposals through the full council. It was not until August 1907 that, through pressure from the Women's Local Government Society (WLGS), women ratepayers were allowed to stand for all local authorities (Hollis 1989: 392, 424).

Even so, women were only gradually elected to councils, experiencing particular difficulties in the great cities, although some with an outstanding reputation won seats in Manchester, Birmingham and Liverpool. Initially, only a few could stand, since to do so they had to be a ratepaying elector (and most women were not). From 1914, this was rectified and all residents became eligible for local elections but, as city council elections were seen as dry runs for parliamentary ones, women were still the last to be chosen. Boroughs, and especially the great cities with their widespread and growing responsibilities, were regarded as 'the glittering prizes of local government' and a magnet to those with political and civic ambitions. They contributed to local economic growth and prosperity and oversaw a growth of professional staff and local regulations alike. As such, they were important in party politics and this could marginalise women, especially as an inner caucus of chairmen – something women were not likely to be before the 1920s – often decided priorities. At the same time, officers now did the individual casework which previously woman had enjoyed on school boards and acted as poor law guardians. There were still areas where women could use such expertise, however, especially as the ever-growing remit of council responsibilities encouraged special-isation, although individuals would often sit on several committees in order to represent their wards' interests (Hollis 1989: 392–6, 398–401, 422–3).

Local government could also fulfil the collective moral imperative promoted in the nineteenth century by T.H. Green and religious leaders such as Canon Barnett, and by the 'civic gospel' promoted in Birmingham by the Nonconformist ministers George Dawson, Robert Dale and Henry Crosskey. Socially concerned men were drawn to these teachings, although condemning the waste of squalor, ignorance and disease as not only costly and inefficient, but cruel, appealed also to those women who had perceived their niche in local affairs as looking after women and children. The rise of 'caring power', with its human-itarian and religious connotations, was reinforced for women in the early twentieth century, both by gendered notions and psychological conclusions drawn from Darwinism and Freud, and by the large expe-rience of many middle-class women in practical philanthropy and voluntary social work. Women had found, however, that whatever their experience and capability, their contribution was often under-valued by men. By the twentieth century, some women, particularly socialists and 'new Liberals', preferred government social welfare to individual charity work: it was more efficient, just and accountable. They hoped, therefore, that as elected councillors they would have greater opportunities for effective service. Whether, indeed, they wished to bring a female voice and expertise into social concerns or achieve political equality (or do both), women increasingly found reasons for seeking some kind of involvement in local government.

From 1902, the area where they were most likely to find this was education (Briggs 1968: 193–206; Hollis 1989: 5–68, 395–6, 398–401, 423–4; Drenth and Haan 1999).

Women on the Birmingham LEA

Birmingham had no women councillors until 1911, when Mrs Ellen Hume Pinsent and Miss Majorie Pugh were elected. From 1913, Miss Clara Martineau began her 17 years' elected service and, by 1920, Birmingham had six women councillors, more than anywhere outside London, which had nine. It was overtaken by Leeds, Liverpool and Sheffield by 1930, but was still one of the top five in 1950. In 1924, for example, Birmingham's nine female councillors comprised about 18 per cent of the local total (CBEC *Report* 1914–24, UBSC; Hollis 1989: 397, 487).

On the other hand, from its inception, Birmingham LEA always appointed at least three co-opted women and, until 1914, had other non-members of the committee regularly in attendance. Many of these, like Mrs Walter Barrow, a non-member from 1903 and then appointed from 1912 to 1924, and Mabel Burrows, co-opted from 1908 to 1928, attended the committee and usually at least two sub-committees for many years. Such women also served as district managers of elementary schools. The sub-committees comprised Elementary and Higher Education (Primary and Secondary after 1945); Technical Education and Evening Schools; Special Schools; Finance and General Purposes; Hygiene (from 1912); and Juvenile Employment and Welfare (from 1930). Except for Finance and General Purposes, there was always at least one woman on each of these. The three most popular sub-committees for women from 1930 to 1944 were Special Schools, Hygiene and Juvenile Employment and Welfare (CBEC *Reports*, UBSC).

It is interesting to see where these women came from and how they got elected. Majorie Pugh and Ellen Pinsent, for example, were able to stand in empty seats in 1911, when Birmingham's wards increased from 18 to 30 after a major boundary extension. Pugh stood as an Independent Liberal in an aldermanic by-election, helped by the WLGS and a strong Birmingham Women's Suffrage Society. Pinsent, elected as a Liberal Unionist, promoted 'efficiency, economy and progress'. Birmingham Liberals at this time were split over Home Rule, with the Kenrick family, for instance, being split down the middle (Hollis 1989: 402, 410).

Throughout most of this period, two members of the Unitarian Kenrick family chaired the committee: George, to 1921, followed by William Byng Kenrick until 1940. Other male councillors and aldermen came from the Unitarian, Quaker and other Nonconformist families that dominated Birmingham's industrial, social and cultural life from the nineteenth century. What has often been ignored is the huge role women of these families played in social, medical and educational work. A large number of the women co-opted, and later elected, to Birmingham LEA were from these families: for example, female members of the Unitarian Beale, Kenrick and Martineau families, the Quaker Barrow, Cadbury and Lloyd families and Congregationalist Dales. Some of these women played a very prominent role both inside and outside the council: Clara Martineau, elected councillor from 1914 to 1932, was later chairman (*sic*) of Special Needs and a Justice of the Peace (JP); Mrs Barrow Cadbury, who became Dame Geraldine, contributed much to the Special Schools Committee over 22 years, also became a JP, founded a remand home and two open-air schools, helped establish juvenile courts for youngsters under 16 (the council remembered her as a very influential member of the Juvenile Employment and Welfare Committee when she died in 1941); her aunt Elizabeth, a JP who was also made a Dame, was a councillor from 1919 to 1924, but actually served on the LEA from 1912 to 1935, her special interests being Hygiene and the School of Art. Known on the council as Mrs George Cadbury, she was chairman of the Hygiene Sub-Committee from its inception in 1911 (CBEC *Minutes* and *Reports*, UBSC; Whitcut 1976: 178–81).

Dame Elizabeth's energetic and humanitarian work for Bournville Village, women's welfare and education and youth work was inspired by her active Quaker faith (Scott 1955; Delamont 2004). In the first years, at least, a number of female Quakers were on the Special Schools Committee, the only one at the time which had as many women on it as men. Many of the female relatives of the Quakers and Unitarians on the committees helped establish and run the multifarious health, welfare and educational schemes for women and children in Birmingham from the late nineteenth century. Julia Lloyd, for example, was co-founder of the Birmingham Nursery School Movement, which was able to start when Mr and Mrs Barrow Cadbury provided the rooms; Alice Beale, who started the Birmingham District Nursing Society, was associated with the Women's Hospital for 63 years and was the first president of the Women's Settlement, established in 1899 as a philanthropic centre working with women and children and supporting systematic training and study on social and industrial welfare. This was founded by the National Union of Women Workers (NUWW) (set up in 1895 and from 1918 known as the National Council of Women), bringing together women, largely middle-class volunteers, engaged in social and civic reform and welfare. Elizabeth Cadbury was honorary treasurer from 1898 to 1907 and president from 1906 to 1907. Birmingham's branch was very strong, full of generations of leading Quaker and Unitarian families. Among their relatives were a growing number of paid professionals. For instance, the second woman doctor in Birmingham and physician at the Women's Hospital for 19 years, Mary Sturge, was from a leading Quaker family. Her grandfather was mayor of Birmingham in the year of her birth (Scott 1955: 81–2; Green 2000: 7–8, 52–9; Pbx7795.s7, *Mary Darby Sturge M.D. Obit. March 14, 1925*: 1–6, UBSC).

Mary Sturge went to Edgbaston High School for Girls, the first secondary school for girls in Birmingham. Established in 1876 by the Unitarians, Quakers and other leading liberals of Birmingham, it was one of many cultural and educational enterprises, also including the Birmingham and Midland Institute and the University, in which they played a big part (Muirhead 1911: 78–82, 175–8, 183, 191, 199–226, 325, 337, 352; Watts 1998a). Many of these schemes emanated from Edgbaston. It was here that Mrs Ellen Pinsent, chairman of the Special Schools Committee from 1903 to 1913 and also on the Hygiene Sub-Committee, came to live after her marriage to a Birmingham solicitor. Her previous experience of practical philanthropy in rural Lincolnshire helped her fit easily with the Edgbaston set of middle-class women who led Birmingham's organised philanthropy. So many of the NUWW were from Edgbaston, indeed, that their list of members was headed by the note 'Where the road only is printed it may be understood that it is in Edgbaston' (Brown 2003: 13).

Women and educational policies

It was in this way that women from wealthy, liberal, progressive families developed their version of the civic gospel. Unitarians and Quakers were the very groups that have been singled out by historians both for their deep interest in science and education and for their progressive views on the role of women (Watts 1998b; Leach 2003). In late nineteenth-century Birmingham, women's rights was an essential aspect of the progressive civic gospel ardently preached by Crosskey in the Unitarian Church of the Saviour, and Unitarian women, supported by male relatives in their tightly knit small elite, were enormously influential both in number and leadership in the local women's suffrage movement (Plant 2000: 721–42). Women councillors in the twentieth century, however, were not necessarily fighting feminist causes, although some, such as Elizabeth Cadbury and Marjorie Pugh, were convinced suffragists (Hollis 1989: 402; Delamont 2004). Nevertheless, most of them did want to ensure a woman's voice was heard, particularly on issues to do with women and children. Pugh's election leaflet, for instance, showed that she believed that women 'lunatics' needed female representation on their management committee, so she spent much time visiting and inspecting lunatic asylums.

So did Miss Burnett, Mrs Pinsent and Clara Martineau. The latter tried to ensure that women, as well as men, could obtain unemployment relief. Amongst other practical measures, the NUWW campaigned for free lavatories for women (Hollis 1989: 427–8, 458).

Generally, however, women on Birmingham Council, especially if they were non-elected, were working within the political and economic positions of their families and class. They were functioning alongside men who were more numerous and held more powerful positions. Their general policies were unlikely to differ much from those of male councillors; they were affected like them by managing the rising cost of local services with trailing government grants and fluctuations in the economy. Like men, some could be more radical or left-wing than others. Miss Pugh, for example, was one who fought for slum clearance and council housing. In a council of property owners she argued, 'The property owners had a right to a fair profit, but a profit which was made on the toll of lives was not a fair profit' (Hollis 1989: 422–3, 448).

It is difficult to tell how far women councillors affected the general educational policies of Birmingham LEA. In the interwar years particularly, retrenchment in the years of a fluctuating economic situation meant that the city slipped behind as an educational leader. The situation was complicated by the fact that there also existed in Birmingham the endowed King Edward VI schools, comprising by 1911 two high schools (one each for boys and girls) and five grammar schools (three for boys and two for girls). These schools were independent of the LEA, but affected the whole system (Hutton 1952: 52ff., 188; Waterhouse 1983b: 11–12; Adams 2004: chapter 3). The Education Committee gave annual scholarships free on merit to pupils from the public elementary schools and to pupils aged between 14 and 16 (later extended to 17 and beyond) to attend or stay on at any council secondary school or a King Edward VI school. The LEA also awarded major scholarships to Birmingham University for pupils who had proceeded to secondary school from one of their elementary schools (CBEC *Report* 1906: 40–6, 60; *Minutes* 1913: 302–5, 692–3, UBSC; Wilson

1911: 554). Although, overall, more boys than girls were awarded scholarships (partly, perhaps, because there were more secondary places for boys), real attempts were made to be more equable. In 1913, for example, it was formally stated that 'Nothing in this Scheme shall bar a girl to the same opportunities for advancement as a boy (except when it is otherwise ruled in the conditions of the gifts or bequest)' (CBEC *Minutes* 1913: 302–5, 692–3, UBSC). This was extremely important in giving girls an opportunity to proceed to Birmingham University, established in 1900 as open to both sexes equally and, indeed, much dependent in its growth on women, especially those reading Arts and hoping to become teachers (Ives *et al.* 2000: 161, 203, 247, 256–65).

Opportunities grew for girls in schooling, therefore, but with gendered overtones, for example in the provision of science and mathematics. As the physical sciences and mathematics grew in importance in twentieth-century schooling, so Birmingham LEA's provision expanded, but it was the boys who had the greater number of practical courses and who were increasingly taught by their own trained class teachers. By 1924, demonstrations to girls were given by five women peripatetic special teachers of hygiene (CBEC *Reports* 1906–15, UBSC; BCC/BH/1/1/1/1-6, Birmingham City Council Archives [BCCA]). This gendered differentiation in what was taught, and how, was reiterated for those girls and boys staying on beyond the age of 14. The boys learnt elementary sciences, especially chemistry and mechanics at first. By 1914 they studied physics and chemistry and had a growing number of laboratories in which to learn these subjects. Girls, on the other hand, learnt domestic science, hygiene and the laws of health, although both sexes could take personal hygiene and nature study (BCC/BH/1/1/1/5, 1907: 8–9, 54–8, 134, BCCA; CBEC *Minutes* 1914: 284–5; 1917: 14, 67; *Reports* 1914–24: 36, UBSC).

This gender differentiation in science was similar in the secondary schools of the council. One of the earliest established, the Central Secondary School in Suffolk Street, was for boys of 12 to 17 only and it concentrated on a modern, general education with specialisation in applied science and engineering. The other boys' secondary schools taught different branches of mathematics, chemistry and physics, but girls were more likely to do just elementary physics and chemistry, followed by biology and hygiene (CBEC *Reports* 1904: 46, 49, 51–2; 1906: 57, 59, 68–9; 1908: 52, UBSC). This difference appears to have continued into the 1920s and 1930s, partly affected by lack of both facilities and employment opportunities (Ives *et al*. 2000: 263; Worsley 2004).

This enthusiasm for domestic science and hygiene, rather than the physical sciences, for girls in upper elementary and secondary education from the working and lower-middle classes, respectively, dated back to the 1890s and was successively reinforced in the twentieth century. It followed national trends and Board of Education encouragement, which extended to secondary schools from the 1920s (Manthorpe 1986: 199–213; Hunt 1991: 22–38, 116–34, 141–3). Admittedly, although boys' grammar schools emphasised physics and chemistry, which were becoming the high-status science subjects of this period, even boys' secondary schools varied in the amount of science they taught, with classics still retaining its elite status (Bishop 1994: 188–9, 192–3, 197). In Birmingham, however, the higher the status of the boys' school, the more and the better the science that was taught. King Edward VI Boys' High School had outstanding mathematical and science scholars from the end of the nineteenth century, from whom came many of the top practitioners of medicine and surgery in Birmingham. The three boys' grammar schools also produced good science scholars, some of whom later became professors at Birmingham University (Wilson 1911: 555; Hutton 1952: 104–5, 161–4, 192, 196, 200; Thomas 1983).

This class difference was seen in the hierarchy of girls' schools despite the general views on women and science. King Edward VI Girls' High had an excellent reputation in science, albeit principally in what were seen as appropriate sciences for girls: physiology and botany. The school won at least two university exhibitions or scholarships annually in these, usually to Cambridge, and had a number of ex-pupils who distinguished themselves in science (Hutton 1952: 181–5; Candler 1971: 80, 82–3, 115; Waterhouse 1983a: 23, 26–8, 32–5, 46, 52). The other King Edward VI girls' schools gradually improved their science facilities too and had some high achievers in medicine, mathematics and other sciences (Wilson 1911: 202–5; Hutton 1952: 202–5; Waterhouse 1983b: 2, 7, 23). Edgbaston High's previous enviable reputation in science, from the end of the nineteenth century, was regained somewhat in the 1930s, although it was not until after the Second World War that there was enough money to build more and better laboratories (a problem in the 1930s for independent, endowed and council schools alike). Many girls went on, however, to take science degrees, resulting in many becoming doctors, nurses and dentists (CBEC *Minutes* 1930: 75, 81–3, 90–106, UBSC; Whitcut 1976: 114, 116–20).

Science in the Birmingham schools thus varied, not only, as might be expected, according to age and the enthusiasm of different teachers, but also in relation to gender and class. The latter two were seen particularly in the technical education promoted so strongly by Birmingham LEA, in line with the interests of local manufacturers. At the top of this was the Municipal Technical School, which thousands of students attended, although mostly as part-timers. The far greater majority of these were males studying different technical and scientific subjects, including electricity, mathematics and electro-chemistry. A tiny minority took advanced classes and qualified in various national examinations or for university places. 'Women's classes' in cookery, dressmaking, laundry and millinery were separate but popular and, by 1914, needed more space, but the 'financial stringency' of the war and post-war years prevented this (BCC/BH1/1/2, 1903–04: 9, 26, 162–5, BCCA; CBEC *Reports* 1903: 51–7; 1906: 67–73; 1907: 60–1; 1909: 58; 1912: 76–7; 1913: 242; 1914: 300–1; 1924–30: 145–6, UBSC). From 1927, the Birmingham Central, Handsworth and Aston technical colleges were recognised as colleges of further education and, by 1939, about 10,000 students attended them. The wide range of science and engineering courses was expanded to include new subjects such as micro-chemistry, opthalmics, aeronautics, microbiology and radio service work. The Birmingham Central Technical College (BCTC) was an approved institution for teaching external degrees in pharmacy for the University of London and other qualifying examinations for chemists from 1927 (CBEC *Reports* 1930–44, UBSC). The strength of the Department of Pharmacy and Biology was good for women since, despite a few brave females in metallurgy and electrical engineering, this was the only scientific area where women began to appear in some numbers. In 1943–4, three of the five degrees in pharmacy went to women, and women also were many of the examinees in other pharmacy examinations and began to be appointed as student demonstrators. A new, well-attended course had started for the London University diploma in nursing and the department noted the increasing demand for physiology up to and at degree level (CBEC, BCTC 1943–4: 2–4, 8–14; *Minutes* 1943: 389; 1944: 394; 1945: 290, UBSC).

Other women did attend BCTC, a huge area of growth being in commercial courses. The domestic science courses, of course, were established specifically for women and, indeed, were increasingly stressed by the late 1930s 'as a factor in maintaining good health' (CBEC *Minutes* 1939: 20–2, 55; BCTC 1943–44: 15–16, UBSC). This chan-nelled girls and women into areas not widely accepted as 'science' and reinforced the idea that 'real' science was not for girls. It was largely class-based too. Similarly, engineering and many applied sciences were often seen as less-estimable subjects by the wealthier in society because they were associated with crafts and manual occupations.

The way the different scientific opportunities for girls worked out in Birmingham thus resonated with general trends of the time, but looking at its provision in some detail is interesting from the point of view of how this might reflect the presence of women on the council. There were usually two women only on each of the Education sub-committees up to the 1940s, although not always even that after-wards. It is not easy to trace individual contributions, but it is unlikely they differed much from the general inclination of the committees in providing almost, but not quite, equal access to secondary education for girls and differentiated scientific education throughout schooling, based on assumed class and gender characteristics and roles. The promotion of science with a domestic bent for girls would fit prevailing views of educating girls almost equally with boys of their class, but, nevertheless, of educating them primarily to be good mothers and housewives. At the same time, it is possible that the women's influence showed in measures like the course in practical sanitation established by the Technical Education and Evening Schools Sub-Committee in 1908, which was designed partly for women to become health visitors (CBEC *Report* 1908: 64, UBSC).

In addition, the scientific interests and the greater educational equality of the elite groups so influential in Birmingham were demonstrated in the top-ranking schools their daughters might attend. The curriculum here gave students the opportunity to take science at university and follow professional careers. For example, roughly just over a third of the female medical students at Birmingham University between 1900 and 1920 were from Birmingham or its nearest neighbours. They were possibly attracted, too, by the fact that the city's hospitals were more open to women medical graduates than most in that period and made a number of appointments of women doctors. The Hospital for Women, the Maternity and Children's hospitals were particularly important in this (*Dean's Register of Students* 1900–19; *Register of Birmingham Medical Graduates and Diplomates* 1905–30, UBSC; *Birmingham Medical Review* [BMR] 1926–39; Dyhouse 2006: 137–54; Waterhouse 1962: 108–15). Many other women doctors went into a new professional opening for women, local government services, and were employed in the School Medical Service by Birmingham LEA (CBEC *Minutes* and *Reports* 1912–44, UBSC). This is shown in the reports of the Hygiene and Special Schools sub-committees, where women had a more decisive role.

Special Schools and Hygiene

The Special Schools and Hygiene sub-committees were the principal ones appointing doctors to work with children and both appointed many women; for example, Dr Caroline O'Connor was superintendent of Special Schools from 1903 to 1915 (BCC/BH/10/1/1/1, BCCA; CBEC *Minutes* 1912, Hygiene, 1, UBSC). The Special Schools Sub-Committee had a succession of woman chairmen, in contrast to general council practice. Ellen Pinsent was even more unusual in chairing a sub-committee as a co-opted member, although as a Liberal Unionist working with the Tories, she did belong to the majority group. Chairman from 1903 to 1913, she has been shown by Anna Brown to have been a dynamic leader. She was involved in both the establishment of special schools and the selection of blind, deaf and 'feebleminded' children for them. As a eugenicist, she feared the 'racial contamination' of the hundreds of mentally handicapped children she found. She separated epileptic children from these and built them a special boarding school. Interestingly, other women councillors preferred children to be in families rather than special boarding schools and disliked her eugenicist views. Pinsent, however, was also a humanitarian and eager to use current educational knowledge to give marginalised children the best care possible. She found funds for special schools and workshops for over a thousand children crippled with tuberculosis, polio, multiple sclerosis and rheumatism. Her chairmanship reveals the power that some women had in Birmingham in education and health (Hollis 1989: 425; Brown 2005: 535–46).

The Hygiene Sub-Committee increasingly took responsibility for the medical health of children as a series of enactments allowed LEAs to do this. For example, from January 1913 it set up a scheme for the dental treatment of schoolchildren in Birmingham schools and, in 1914, appointed the first of a small number of women dentists. The range of treatments given to schoolchildren expanded with increasing medical knowledge and with legislation on both prevention and treatment of infectious and mental diseases and various childhood ailments. Women played a crucial role in running the committees in Birmingham, creating and managing policies, appointing the doctors, dentists and, of course, nurses. Some of the science subjects promoted for girls offered a prime way into these public health services at all levels (CBEC *Minutes* 1913: 588–92; 1914: 452; 1915: 115, 312; 1917: 107, 246; *Reports* 1914–24: 59–72; 1924–30: 75–81; 1930–45, UBSC).

Birmingham was divided into districts, each with an assistant school medical officer (SMO) and one SMO overall. These SMOs ran the school, dental, aural and ophthalmic clinics, and attended three hospitals and specialist provision including children's homes and a variety of special, residential, day and open-air schools (*BMR* 1935: 33–5; CBEC *Medical Report* 1937: 3–4, 19–21, UBSC). Many of the assistant SMOs were women doctors (33 between 1931 and 1944). In 1938, for instance, eight of the 14 assistant SMOs were women. The close cooperation between the School Medical and the Public Health departments was exemplified in the empirical research on malnutrition by some women doctors in 1936–7, leading to a range of suggested remedies, including the teaching of cookery and hygiene in schools. The inspections of the SMOs were followed up by the school nurses both in schools and through home visits to the children. Detailed statistics enabled a more scientific approach to the management of public health (CBEC *Medical Reports* 1937: 6–9, 18–20, 38; 1938: 4, 7–13; 1940: 4, UBSC).

Some provision mixed medical and social care, for example the Child Guidance Clinic, of which the committee was very proud. Established in 1932, particularly in response to the urgings of the National Council for Women in Birmingham, the clinic employed a number of women, including an increasing number of female medical psychiatrists (CBEC *Minutes* 1931: 59–60, 96; 1934: 427–9; 1941: 313; 1943: 351; 1944: 332, 366–7; *Report on the Child Guidance Clinic* 1938: 1–6; *Medical Report* 1937: 8–9).

In many years, not only a third to a half of the members, but also the chairmen of the Hygiene and Special Schools sub-committees were women. It was these committees which appointed the female doctors and medical personnel who treated and managed women and children in the educational and medical institutions which women of the governing elite in Birmingham had helped set up.

Conclusion

It can be seen, therefore, that, although circumscribed by both regulations and assumptions of their time, women, both elected and non-elected, played an important role on the Birmingham Education Committee. Many of them were from religious and social groups that had dominated Birmingham at the end of the nineteenth century. The women brought to their council work expertise and aspirations derived from their charitable and sometimes professional work outside. Their contribution can be seen principally in the committees most concerned with the welfare of children, an area that was becoming increasingly significant in government in the twentieth century.

References

Adams, D. (2004) 'From consensus to conflict? Continuity and change in the structure of provision for secondary education in Birmingham, 1902–2002'. Unpublished MPhil thesis, University of Birmingham.

Bishop, G. (1994) *Eight Hundred Years of Physics Teaching*. Basingstoke: Fisher Miller.

Briggs, A. (1968; first edition 1963) *Victorian Cities*. Harmondsworth: Penguin.

Brown, A. (2003) 'Private lives and public policy: Ellen Pinsent, special education and welfare in Birmingham, 1900–1913'. Unpublished MA dissertation, University of Birmingham.

— (2005) 'Ellen Pinsent: including the "feebleminded" in Birmingham, 1900–1913', *History of Education*, 34(5), 535–46.

Candler, W.I. (1971) *King Edward VI High School for Girls, Birmingham. Part I 1883–1925*. London: Ernest Benn.

Delamont, S. (2004) 'Cadbury, Dame Elizabeth Mary (1858–1951)'. In *Oxford Dictionary of National Biography*. Oxford: Oxford University Press.

Drenth, A. van and Haan, Francisca de (1999) *The Rise of Caring Power: Elizabeth Fry and Josephine Butler in Britain and the Netherlands.* Amsterdam: Amsterdam University Press

Dyhouse, C. (2006) *Students: A gendered history.* London: Routledge.

Eyken, Willem van der (ed.) (1973) *Education, the Child and Society: A documentary history, 1900–1973.* Harmondsworth: Penguin.

Goodman, J. and Harrop, S. (eds) (2000) *Women, Educational Policy-making and Administration in England: Authoritative women since 1880.* London: Routledge.

Green, M.D. (2000) *Images of England. Birmingham women.* Stroud: Tempus Publishing.

Hollis, P. (1989; first edition 1987) *Ladies Elect: Women in English local government, 1865–1914.* Oxford: Oxford University Press.

Hunt, F. (1991) *Gender and Policy in English Education, 1902–1944.* Hemel Hempstead: Harvester Wheatsheaf.

Hutton, T.W. (1952) *King Edward's School Birmingham, 1552–1952.* Oxford: Basil Blackwell.

Ives, E., Drummond, D. and Schwarz, L. (2000) *The First Civic University: Birmingham, 1880–1980: An introductory history.* Birmingham: University of Birmingham Press.

Jenkins, E.W. and Swinnerton, B. (1998) *Junior School Science Education in England and Wales since 1900: From steps to stages.* London: Woburn Press.

Leach, C. (2003) 'Quaker women and education from the late eighteenth to the mid nineteenth century'. Unpublished PhD thesis, University College, Winchester.

Manthorpe, C. (1986) 'Science or domestic science? The struggle to define an appropriate education for girls in early twentieth-century England'. *History of Education*, 15(3), 195–213.

Martin, J. (1999) *Women and the Politics of Schooling in Victorian and Edwardian England.* London: Leicester University Press.

Muirhead, J.H. (ed.) (1911) *Birmingham Institutions: Lectures given at the university.* Birmingham: Cornish Brothers.

Plant, H. (2000) '"Ye are all one in Christ Jesus": aspects of Unitarianism and feminism in Birmingham, c. 1869–90'. *Women's History Review*, 9(4), 721–42.

Scott, R. (1955) *Elizabeth Cadbury, 1858–1951.* London: George G. Harrap.

Thomas, D.I. (ed.) (1983) *King Edward VI Camp Hill School for Boys, 1883–1903.* Redditch: King Edward VI's Foundation.

Waterhouse, R. (1962) *Children in Hospital. A hundred years of childcare in Birmingham.* London: Hutchinson.

— (1983a) *King Edward VI High School for Girls, 1883–1983.* Redditch: King Edward VI's Foundation.

— (1983b) 'Introduction'. In *Six King Edward Schools, 1883–1983.* Birmingham: King Edward VI's Foundation.

Watts, R. (1998a) 'From lady teacher to professional: a case study of some of the first headteachers of girls' secondary schools in England'. *Educational Management and Administration*, 26(4), 339–51.

— (1998b) *Gender, Power and the Unitarians in England, 1760–1860.* London: Longman.

Whitcut, J. (1976) *Edgbaston High School, 1876–1976.* Birmingham: published by the Governors.

Wilson, R.G. (1911) 'The schools of King Edward VI'. In J.H. Muirhead (ed.) *Birmingham Institutions: Lectures given at the university.* Birmingham: Cornish Brothers.

Worsley, M. (2004) 'A history of Roman Catholic education in Birmingham'. Unpublished PhD thesis, University of Birmingham.

5 Policy formation and the work of His Majesty's Inspectorate, 1918–45

Peter Gordon

Historians of education have written extensively on the activities of His/Her Majesty's Inspectorate (HMI) since its inception in 1839. These studies have been mainly concerned either with the period leading to the 1902 Education Act or the post-war policies pursued after the 1944 Education Act. Little attention has so far been paid to the crucial interwar period when the service twice underwent reorganisation. This chapter is an attempt to fill this gap. It also reflects two of Richard Aldrich's interests: the importance of historical perspectives on current educational policy, and the role of the Inspectorate. These themes were clearly represented in our collaborative writings over the years, particularly *Education and Policy in England in the Twentieth Century* (Gordon *et al.* 1991).

By the end of the First World War, the Inspectorate, like the rest of the education system, had been much altered in its personnel and functions. The appointment of inspectors (HMI) had been suspended by the Board of Education during wartime and many staff were seconded to other departments. Full inspections had been halted and HMI were employed in such tasks as advising local education authorities (LEAs) wishing to appeal against the military conscription of 'indispensable' teachers and helping schools suffering from staff shortages ('Circulars and memoranda, 1915' file, ED 22/15, National Archives [NA]).

Within the Inspectorate, however, there was a much greater problem to be tackled. The Education Bill which preceded the 1918 'Fisher' Act sought ambitiously to provide better and longer educational experiences for the majority of the school population. The school-leaving age was to be raised to 14, with a view to increasing it to 15, and the half-time system was to be abolished. Those not attending full-time schooling until 16 were to undertake part-time education, based on the German model, for 320 hours a year. Fees were to be abolished in all public elementary schools, higher-grade elementary schools were recommended and LEAs were charged with making adequate provision for advanced and practical instruction by means of central schools or special classes, as well as creating full-time junior trade and technical schools. More powers were given under the Act to the Board of Education and LEAs were required to submit schemes to the Board for approval (Sherington 1981: 119–20).

The reasons for the Act's comparative failure, notably the opposition from LEAs and employers, as well as the post-war economic recession, do not concern us here, but the immediate impact on the Inspectorate was soon apparent. After receiving the Royal Assent, in August 1918, discussions soon focused on how the Inspectorate might effectively facilitate the day continuation schools specified in the Act. The Board identified a need for increased numbers of inspectors 'with qualifications in humanistic subjects and a knowledge of (and if possible a first hand acquaintance with) the industrial and social conditions under which young people live and work'. Nine inspectors would be required for this work: four men and five women. The expansion of all forms of technical instruction, especially for commerce, building, mining and the chemical industries, would require a further three inspectors, all of whom would be men ('The 1918 Act: Organisation', minute, 19 November 1918, ED 23/138, NA).

The 1918 Act also necessitated the reorganisation of HMI. Five branches of the Inspectorate had been established in 1902: elementary, secondary, technological, teacher training and medical, as well as a separate woman inspectorate. Now that LEAs were required to draw up a comprehensive scheme covering the whole field of education, there was a need for greater coordination within the Inspectorate in order to offer sound advice. The outcome was the establishment of divisional committees comprising inspectors in all three branches of the Board in each of the nine divisions into which England was divided for inspection purposes. Each committee appointed a district inspector (DI) to act as its secretary and to keep records of the fortnightly meetings (Selby-Bigge to Fisher, 11 December 1918, ED 23/136, NA). Questions concerning staffing, equipment and premises were now left largely to the DI, involving much additional clerical work and an obligation to act as spokesman for his colleagues at divisional committees. In remembering the late chief inspector, elementary branch, F.H.B. Dale, a colleague and historian of the Inspectorate, attributed his death to 'the heavy burden in connection with the 1918 Education Act' (Boothroyd 1923: 57).

The dramatic post-war economic crisis led the Cabinet, in December 1920, to suspend all schemes involving expenditure and the raising of the school-leaving age was also postponed. In August of the following year, the Lloyd George government appointed a committee to advise on ways of reducing expenditure by 30 per cent. The Geddes Committee Report, published in February 1922, recommended an £18 million reduction, encompassing cuts in teachers' salaries and the abandonment of plans for day continuation schools and further free places in secondary schools.

At an early stage, the Inspectorate was mobilised to support officials of the Board in the hope of countering the worst effects of possible cuts (Savage 1983: 261–80). The Chief Inspector for Secondary Schools W.C. Fletcher circulated his colleagues, requesting them to gather material for the president for the defence of expenditure on secondary education. He wrote,

> We can easily get together statistics in the Office but should be glad
> to have something more detailed and intimate. I think that if each
> inspector whose experience goes back to pre-war days would take
> some small area tolerably well known to him and make a pretty full
> comparison of its higher educational state now and as he formally
> knew, we might get something more useful than mere statistics.

Suggested areas included salaries, qualifications of staff, late entrants, early school leavers and schools' precarious financial positions. Fletcher concluded, 'Generally speaking, we want to show that there is a new attitude towards education' (W.C. Fletcher, 'Expenditure on Secondary Education', 1 February 1921, Memoranda to Inspectors file, S.380, ED 22/49, NA). HMI were also to be proactive in seeking out possible overstaffing in secondary schools, and for the better use of part-time teachers. Where substantial economies could be affected, the HMI should report them to the Board (note by E.H. Pelham, 11 May 1922, Memoranda to Inspectors file, S.418, ED 22/126, NA).

Fisher, in considering economies 'without impairing educational efficiency', consulted H.M. Richards, chief inspector, elementary branch. Richards suggested that in more affluent neighbourhoods it might be possible to teach children under 6 on a part-time basis. 'It has always been my opinion,' he wrote, 'that two or three hours in school was quite enough for very young children. . . . No well to do parent will send his children under six years of age for the hours now enforced in Public Elementary Schools.' He also suggested that staff could be more economically used if the older children were allowed to work by themselves (note by Richards, 10 May 1921, Memoranda to Inspectors file, E.211, ED 22/21, NA).

Ways of saving money also fell on the Inspectorate itself. From 1918, DIs had been provided with free telephones in their homes, which were virtually their offices, in order to save time in travelling and in communicating with LEAs and the Board. Now, individual DIs were asked to justify whether the payment for the telephone was a valid charge on public funds (Memoranda to Inspectors file, E.212, S388, 5 June 1921, ED 22/21, NA). Travel also came under scrutiny:

inspectors would no longer operate outside their own area. Instead, DIs were expected to take on this extra burden (Board of Education, 'Modification and Arrangements for Inspectors', 14 November 1921, ED 22/49, NA). The damage inflicted on schools and the Inspectorate was extensive. In November 1922, a coalition government was defeated at the general election, to be replaced by a Conservative administration. Fisher's grandiose plans for educational advance were to be long delayed.

The reorganisation of the Inspectorate in the 1920s reflected the changes in education generally. The personnel, too, were divided into a number of categories, each articulating differences in background and standing of members of the service. A typical view was expressed by one of the many Oxbridge men who formed the majority of the officials of the Board. Sir Edmund Phipps, principal assistant secretary, elementary branch, wrote,

> It is essential that they [the Inspectorate] should contain a large proportion of men of recognised ability. Honours at the Universities are not the only criterion for the purpose, but broadly speaking, they make the standard most readily applied. All "first class" men don't make good Inspectors. But until the "first class" candidates are exhausted, strong reasons are required for taking the "second class".
>
> (Phipps to Richards, 15 October 1920, ED 23/608, NA)

Lack of personal experience in teaching in elementary schools accounted for the poor relationship between such inspectors and teachers (Maclure 2000: xxiii).

The first move away from this philosophy occurred in 1921, with the merging into one grade of assistant inspectors who had had long experience of teaching in elementary schools, sub-inspectors, 'a moribund body and the Cinderella of the subordinate class', and junior inspectors, founded in 1901, mainly for university graduates ('Memorandum submitted by Sub-Inspectors with reference to improved scale of salary and pension', 1920, ED 23/608, NA). All worked in the elementary branch at lower rates than full HMI. Under the new system, some were later promoted to full inspectorships.

At this time, each branch worked under a chief inspector (CI) and a chief woman inspector (CWI). The elementary, secondary and technological inspectorates also operated under a DI in each of the nine separate divisions in England. Additionally, there were some 17 staff inspectors with national responsibility for special types of work or individual subjects. A brief 1925 minute in the Board of Education records gives the first indications of change in official thinking. Addressed to CI Richards, it begins, 'This is the sort of idea I was beginning to work on for a unified Inspectorate'. Phipps envisaged a structure based on geographical counties, containing HMIs from all three branches. An alternative plan was for groupings of not more than seven divisions corresponding to those of assistant secretaries (Phipps to Richards, 'Note on the Inspectorate', 1925, ED 23/604, NA). Circular 1382, dated 21 July 1926, set out the proposed changes. A unified Inspectorate under a senior chief inspector (SCI) (Richards) was to coordinate the work of the Inspectorate as a whole, whilst retaining his CI responsibilities (Lawton and Gordon 1987: 129). As the separate elementary, secondary and technological branches of the Board had been abolished in 1922, HMI needed to reflect this change. Under the SCI, the three CIs acted as expert advisers to the Board, forming an unofficial cabinet. The CWI was also responsible to the SCI. Each of the nine divisions had one DI who linked together all forms of educational activity; the staff inspectors were deployed by SCI on either specialist work or with the Department of Special Inquiries. Women staff inspectors, one for each division, acted under the DI. By 1930, with the phasing out of the teacher training and medical branches, the reorganisation was completed.

The Board of Education Inspectors' Association was most concerned, however. Founded in 1919, it represented all ranks, with a membership of around 300 to 400. The Association had been consulted by the Board on the proposals and had proposed some amendments. Whilst generally welcoming the new structure set out in Circular 1382, it was anxious about the position of older and senior inspectors: DIs over the age of 45 were thought to have slimmer chances of gaining promotion, for example (HMI F.W. Chambers to Sir Aubrey Symonds, 12 December 1925, ED 24/1675, NA).

The question of HMI salaries had long been contentious. As early as 1918, an educational journal commented that 'The emoluments of the inspectorial service have now become so meagre in view of the high cost of living that they will have to be considerably improved in order to attract the best type of teacher' (*Journal of Education*, 592, 1 November 1918: 684). The Board was sympathetic to this view and appealed to the Treasury for improvement. The situation was especially serious in the secondary Inspectorate. HMI were usually expected to have a first-class honours degree and to have held posts of some responsibility before joining the service. A petition to CI Pullinger by three technological branch inspectors, in February 1919, pointed out that the general level of remuneration had remained unchanged for many years. The salaries of directors of education for counties and large cities were, in several cases, twice those paid to DIs, and in some cases exceeded that paid to any officer of the Board. It was anomalous, they argued, that the Inspectorate now had the task of advising and supervising those in receipt of salaries higher than their own, and, quoting the words of one director, 'An HMI is not what he was' (W. Pullen, A. Harris and C.H. Cressey to Pullinger, 23 February 1919, ED 23/608, NA).

The technological Inspectorate also experienced difficulties in recruiting and retaining those with expert qualifications. Writing in 1925, CI Abbott noted that, since the war, a number of outstanding men had left the service: among others, J. Dover Wilson to a professorship of education at King's College, London, F.F. Potter to the post of director of Education for Cheshire and F.H. Spencer, now chief inspector for the London County Council (LCC). Selby-Bigge, permanent secretary to the Board of Education, agreed that something should be done, 'but the Treasury has been rather sticky in this matter' (Abbott to M.G. Holmes, 24 March 1926; Selby-Bigge to M.G. Holmes, 25 March 1926, ED 26/338, NA).

Another issue, which was prominent after 1918, was the aggregation of women in the Inspectorate. Since Robert Morant, the first permanent secretary, had created the post of CWI in 1905, the small staff of women HMI had grown steadily. However, the majority were employed in the inspection of domestic subjects and younger children, with few recruited for secondary school inspection. Fisher observed in 1919 that there were no women in the list submitted to him by the Inspectorate for vacancies in this field. He considered that there should be a noticeable increase in women inspectors in view of the large number of girls' schools inspected and asked the CI for secondary schools, Fletcher, for his views. Fletcher defended the status quo on the grounds that vacancies had been caused by the death and promotion of DIs: 'Hitherto, District Inspectors have always been men, and it seems to me that for the present at least this must continue to be the case. At all levels, no hint to the contrary had been made to me and I took it to be the case' (Fletcher to Fisher, 1 April and 3 April 1919, ED 23/846, NA). However, some progress had been made in filling senior posts. Women staff inspectors had been allocated to each Inspectorate branch and, by 1926, there were 11 female staff inspectors; but there remained glaring inequalities and anomalies in the pay scales of men and women.

The main grievance of the women inspectors was the lack of opportunity to undertake interesting and responsible work. Some openly resented being subservient to the DIs, not always with fortunate outcomes (Gordon 1988: 193–207). Working almost entirely in the elementary sector, they were rarely consulted on proposals put forward by LEAs for buildings or school reorganisation. Similarly, information or views to be conveyed to LEAs by women were almost invariably channelled through their male colleagues and women were excluded from attending annual divisional conferences.

In 1921, the Report of the Royal Commission on the Civil Service urged the Board to implement a system of complete aggregation as soon as possible. Selby-Bigge expressed doubts about this procedure. 'Suspicion of divided responsibility,' he wrote, 'would alarm HMI and lead to confusion in the Board' (minute by Selby-Bigge, 7 August 1923, ED 22/846, NA). This assessment was correct: one secondary male HMI wrote to his DI colleague:

> Now the policy of Unity in the Inspectorate makes it desirable to avoid anything in the Inspectorate that might be interpreted as proclaiming a different status for E and S Women. Apart from this policy of unity, there are the special circumstances of the present time and the practical certainty of misunderstanding if not misrepresentation while otherwise competent women are content to subordinate their judgment to the will of a few acidulated spinsters, masking an inferiority complex by a parade of devotion to "Principle".
>
> (E.J.R. Bridge to F.B. Stead, 2 November 1925, ED 22/138, NA)

The unification of the Inspectorate, in 1926, placed the CWI on a level with the other three CIs. The increase in the number of women inspectors to the secondary branch went some way to meeting the demand for more responsibility, though even then they were assigned mainly to girls' schools (Memoranda to Inspectors file, S.373, June 1929, ED 22/138, NA).

Witnesses appearing before the 1929–30 Royal Commission on the Civil Service confirmed the view that the system should remain much as it was. G.T. Hankin, secretary of the Inspectors' Association, stated that he considered women less able to do administrative work than men:

> At the present moment I feel that the education of women, as a whole, has not given them the chance to acquire the power of doing the sort of semi-administrative work . . . with the same ease as men. . . . It is very much easier for a man than it is for a woman to go and smoke a pipe with a director of education and discuss matters with him in an informal way.

He added, 'a good many men do not find it so easy to sit down and gossip with a woman as they do with a man' (Royal Commission on the Civil Service, 1929–30, Q. 8936–7). The evidence given by the former and first CWI, the Hon. Dame Maude Lawrence, daughter of a previous Viceroy of India, did not help the case for women inspectors. She advocated the need for segregation, rather than aggregation, in women inspectors' work. She also supported the continuance of the marriage ban, which required women to hand in their resignation on marriage, though she admitted that she had 'no experience of how far the matrimonial state leads to contentment'. She also agreed with the statement that the double strain of home interests and of work might be too much for them (ibid., Q. 14995 and 15012).

The Royal Commission recommendation that the staff of men and women inspectorates should be aggregated led to the establishment of a Board committee, chaired by Sir Henry Pelham, now permanent secretary, in March 1932. It rapidly accepted the Commission's recommendations as policy, with women's salary scales fixed at around 80 per cent of their male colleagues (Pelham to Sir Donald Maclean, President of the Board, 24 May 1932, ED 24/676, NA). Although the women inspectors were retained as a separate corps, their functions were widened. In 1933 women were appointed as district inspectors in the elementary and secondary branches, and the first woman divisional inspector was appointed three years later. The Treasury approved a revised establishment for the English Inspectorate on the basis of complete aggregation from April 1938. The force now consisted of: a SCI, 2 CIs, a CWI, 9 divisional inspectors, 19 staff inspectors, 162 HMI and 12 assistant inspectors (R.S. Wood, 'Establishment Minute No. 1447. Inspectorate: New Establishment'. 7 January 1935, ED 23/344, NA). With the retirement of Miss A.G. Philip, in 1938, the title of HM CWI was changed to Senior Woman Inspector (Lawton and Gordon 1987: 99).

A major issue, which brought the Inspectorate and the Board into dispute, was its autonomy. In 1922, Selby-Bigge questioned whether too much emphasis was being placed on full inspections, suggesting to Fletcher, the CI of secondary schools, that more time should be spent on inspecting below-average schools, and that reports should be less elaborate, but more critical. Fletcher, in his reply, vigorously defended the Inspectorate's policy, declaring, 'I think that reliance can very safely be placed on the general knowledge of their schools possessed by the

District Inspector' (Rhodes 1981: 102). Richards, the SCI, was also exasperated by what he regarded as 'ill-informed criticisms' (Memoranda to Inspectors file, E.253, 17 January 1923, ED 22/28, NA).

Elementary schools had been relieved of regular inspections after the ending of payment-by-results in 1895, but secondary schools were subject to more routine inspections. In 1922, the president of the Board, Fisher, decided to increase the interval between full inspections of secondary schools from five to ten years, in order to allow HMI time for more subject inspections (Memoranda to Inspectors file, S.407, 12 April 1922, ED 22/126, NA). By 1936, LEAs were complaining of the length of intervals between inspections as well as the 30 per cent reduction in time given to routine inspections. F.R.G. Duckworth, the SCI, protested to one of the assistant secretaries about the extra strain being put on a modest-sized Inspectorate at a time when there were many other resourcing pressures. In his case for the augmentation of the service, Duckworth gives an insight into the nature of the widespread demands placed on HMI since 1918. Apart from the growing number of secondary schools to be visited, short courses run by HMI for teachers had expanded in scope and number. The 'panel system', whereby groups of eight or nine inspectors investigated particular problems or collected information, was time-consuming. Other demands were for supervising the 'special place' examinations system, participating in preparing education booklets of various kinds, including the *Handbook of Suggestions* and of mounting special inquiries, for example into homework, the raising of the school-leaving age and the employment of foreign assistance. In spite of Duckworth's plea, the Inspectorate size was only marginally increased (Duckworth to N.D. Bosworth Smith, 10 November 1936, ED 23/712, NA).

Inspectors were also heavily involved in providing information to committees set up to examine possible educational reform, and in following up LEAs' implementation of national policy. When the Spens Report on secondary education was published in 1938, inspectors were ordered to report on possibilities for suitable associations between grammar and modern schools. The Inspectorate was also heavily involved in the work of the Norwood Committee on Curriculum and Examinations in Secondary Schools (Lawton and Gordon 1987: 60) from inception. According to G.G. Williams, a principal assistant secretary, a suitable person – HMI R.H. Barrow was eventually selected – for the key post of secretary to the Norwood Committee could 'only be found in one of H M Inspectors' (Williams to Maurice Holmes, Permanent Secretary, 17 December 1940, ED 12/476, NA). When it was published in 1943, the Norwood Report praised HMI as 'the eyes and ears of the Board' (Board of Education 1943: 51). A good example of HMI involvement in policy-making can also be seen in the deliberations of the Board of Education committee which produced the 'Green Book', *Education After the War*, in 1941. Besides senior Board officials, two CIs and the SWI were committee members (Gosden 1976: 238–9).

By the outbreak of the Second World War, the size of the Inspectorate had diminished, from 383 in 1922 to 348. While deaths and retirements reduced the service still further, no wartime replacements were made. Moreover, 25 HMI and 13 assistant inspectors were seconded to other government departments (minute, 16 January 1941, ED 23/714, NA) and few reductions were made in the scope of existing HMI duties (Dunford 1998: 19–23). Although full inspections were suspended, over half the Inspectorate's time was occupied with such tasks as surveys of evacuee billeting and the provision of education in reception areas (Memoranda to Inspectors file, S.634, 17 October 1939, ED 22/214, NA). The drift back to urban centres, as the war proceeded, also demanded action.

Another matter requiring resolution was the relationship between HM Inspectorate, the Board and the LCC, which had its own inspectorate, staffed by highly qualified men and women whose salaries compared well with those of HMI. Sir Robert Blair, LCC education officer, and F.H.B. Dale had reached a concordat in 1912, whereby the inspection of elementary schools in London was left to the London inspectorate, with HM Inspectorate confining its attention to subject reports on these schools. As a result, the HM Inspectorate had reduced its staff in London (Christian 1922: 159).

With the new Education Bill looming, the Inspectorate made the first move. R.H. Charles, CI, elementary branch, in a long minute to the president, R.A. Butler, commented,

> It is not too much to say that the idea that LCC schools were so good that they needed no inspection by the Board, has been dissipated in the eyes of Local Authorities, and many teachers in the country generally ask the question, 'Why does not the Board inspect London?' has been widely asked [*sic*].
>
> > (Richards, 'Inspection of Elementary Schools in London', 18 August 1942, ED 23/667, NA)

Charles had been a member of the Board's team, headed by Sir Maurice Holmes, the permanent secretary, the SCI, Duckworth, and W. Elliott, CI, technical branch, which met in April 1943 with two London officials, Graham Savage, LCC education officer, and the capital's chief inspector, Dr John Brown (Maclure 1990: 147). Under the Bill, the term 'elementary' disappeared and full-time education would be divided into primary and secondary at the age of 11. This 'would render the 1912 concordat nugatory and the Board Inspectors for their part stood to benefit from the experience derived from the inspection of London County Council' (Minutes, 19 April 1943, ED 23/ 667, NA). Savage, who had been SCI from 1932 to 1940, before joining the LCC, told Holmes a few days later 'that the mere effluxion of time is in itself sufficient justification for a suggestion that the whole position should now be examined' (Savage to Holmes, 27 March 1943, ED 23/667, NA). Butler took a personal interest in the question of the Board's inspectors operating in the London area. Charles Robertson, chairman of the London Education Committee, conceded that there would be no political or other difficulties 'so long as certain [LCC] officials would still be described as "Inspectors"' (Robertson to Butler, 25 June 1943, ED 26/667, NA).

At this point, the advice of Mr F. Bray, a principal assistant secretary, proved decisive. He advised Butler,

> In normal circumstances it would be almost impossible for the Board to take the step proposed by Mr Robertson without an official enquiry

and a good deal of mud slinging. But with a definite promise from the 'Inner Cabinet' not to offer opposition, this 'chance in a lifetime' of getting back our right of inspection should not be missed. In my view a letter to the L.C.C. should (1) omit criticism of past work of their Inspectorate, if only because the L.C.C. are so very 'touchy' on questions concerned with the efficiency or otherwise of their staff and (2) inform the L.C.C. that we propose to undertake the duty of assessing the work of the Schools.

Bray believed that the assessment by the Inspectorate 'seems to offer the best contribution the Board can make' (Bray to R.A. Butler, 21 July 1943, ED 23/667, NA). In early August, Butler informed Robertson, 'I am convinced it would be to the mutual advantage of London education and of the national system of education if the inspection of elementary schools in London by HMI were resumed' (Butler to Robertson, 11 August 1943, ED 23/667, NA). In spite of opposition from Brown on behalf of his inspectors, as well as from many teachers, HMI gradually re-established their involvement with London inspection.

The reassessment of the relationships between HMI and the LCC was largely the result of the many new duties to be imposed on the Inspectorate by the impending Education Bill. However, of even more moment was the need to establish the position of HMI in relation to the Board's officials. In April 1944, a new SCI, Martin Roseveare, had been appointed on Duckworth's retirement. A vigorous and out-spoken defender of the Inspectorate, he immediately clashed with the equally forceful director of Establishments, R.J. Finny. In May, Finny had written on the need for the Inspectorate and the Board to understand each other. Roseveare replied:

> Of course I entirely agree that they should do so, nothing could be more desirable. On the other hand, I have already plenty of evidence in my papers to support the view . . . that this needs careful handling. At the present moment, there is a tendency . . . for all sorts of Branches or Sections in the Office to regard HMI as simply their outside man. . . . This leads to the danger that the wretched Inspector may have anything up to a dozen masters apparently, and this seems to me all wrong. All these headquarter folk have a particular furrow to plough

and cannot be expected to realise the whole burden which lies upon HMI. Not only that, but if you add the activities of all these separate Departments together and their impact upon HMI, the total should still only influence a fraction, certainly less than half of his life, because his main job is to inspect schools and teaching.

I want us to be quite clear on one point: that the boss of HMIs is SCI, together with his CI colleagues. I cannot imagine what SCI's job is meant to be unless it is this. It must be up to SCI not only to know the whole general burden which falls upon HMIs, but to be in a position to influence that burden by such contact with the other branches of the office that unsuitable jobs are not thrown out at him. I want to make this perfectly clear, that this in no way conflicts with the desirability of HMIs knowing other folk in the Office and working very harmoniously with them.

(Roseveare to R.J. Finny, 14 May 1944, ED 23/714, NA)

The correspondence between the two men continued. Roseveare, in apologising for 'the bombardment on this theme', claimed that Finny saw no need for the Inspectorate 'to have more than an odd clerk or two' and listed some of the additional duties now facing HMI: reporting and encouraging new educational developments, post-war training schemes for the army, supervising the emergency (teacher) training scheme, and the training of teaching personnel following the McNair Report, organising teachers' courses, and dealing with the resumed full inspection programme (Roseveare to Finny, 24 May 1944, ED 23/714, NA). In a further letter, he added, 'I am very perturbed by the dire need of more Inspectors at once and I feel we can hardly wait for the machine to turn to produce more bodies' (Roseveare to Finny, 15 June 1944, ED 23/714, NA).

Roseveare headed a committee of HMI and Board officials to investigate the future needs of the Inspectorate, which reported in July 1944. Many of his suggested reforms were accepted. The report showed that the education system – now regarded as a singly unified one for which the minister was responsible – should be reflected in the pattern of the Inspectorate. HMI was to be a single body, under the control of a full-time SCI, with separate and individual internal bodies avoided. The distinction between elementary and secondary branches was abolished and women inspectors were now known as HMI. The grade of assistant inspector also disappeared. The number of CIs was increased from three to six and divisional inspectors gained in status. Roseveare's case for an increase in the Inspectorate had been well argued. In 1945 there were 364 inspectors: by 1949 it had risen to 527, though full aggregation had to wait until 1961, when equal pay for men and women was achieved.

One other longstanding source of friction between the Board and HMI was the continuing claim of the Inspectorate for its independence. The appointment of inspectors by the Crown and the title of HMI had almost disappeared in 1902, but Robert Morant had been persuaded to preserve the distinctive title on the grounds that LEAs were now appointing their own inspectorates (Phipps to H.E. Boothroyd, 23 November 1923, ED 23/271, NA). Forty years later, Finny questioned whether the title should be continued, reflecting the prevalent office view that the autonomy of the Inspectorate could be a hindrance to policy formation and eroded the power of officials. Indeed, Finny called this method of appointment 'something of an anachronism', because

> Inspectors, whether HMIs or not, are to all intents and purposes officers of the Department and *not* independent of it. There may have been in the distant past differences of outlook, but the tendency has been, so far as my experience goes, to bring the Inspectors and the office staff into much closer and more intimate relationship and the core of Inspectors has become more an integral part of the Board's staff.

Finny concluded that there were two courses open: either to discontinue the title altogether or to alter the method of appointment. In his opinion, appointments to the Inspectorate should rest entirely with the president, having before him recommendations of a selection board (Finny to Wood, 17 June 1944, ED 23/669, NA).

By contrast, the Norwood Report of the previous year had firmly supported HMI independence on the grounds that

> There must be a guarantee to the nation in any real democratic system that the business of the schools is education, and that it is being carried out in freedom according to the ideals and methods which are proper to it. They must therefore themselves be recognised as men and women who in important problems are expected to exercise an independent judgment and to be free to say what they think. Just in order to emphasise this claim and this responsibility we feel that the Inspectorate should continue to be known as His Majesty's Service.
>
> (Board of Education 1943: 51)

Finny admitted to the deputy secretary, Sir Robert Wood, the strength of this argument. Whilst believing it to be 'rather an overstatement of the idea of independence of HM Inspectors which may underlie the method of appointment [nevertheless] it brings out the distinction between Inspectors and other officers of the Board'. No further action on this issue was attempted (Finny to Wood, 17 June 1944, ED 23/669, NA).

The interwar Inspectorate was under intensive pressure to change the nature of its operations in order to respond to new educational challenges. It successfully survived internal reorganisation to cope with legislative demands, whilst at the same time successfully defending its long cherished independence from both politicians and Board officials. With the coming of the 1944 Education Act, the Inspectorate was in good shape to assume the many responsibilities given to it under the Act.

References

Board of Education (1943) *Curriculum and Examinations in Secondary Schools* (Norwood Report). London: HMSO.

Boothroyd, H.E. (1923) *A History of the Inspectorate*. London: Board of Inspectors' Association.

Christian, G.A. (1922) *English Education and Inspection*, London: Wallace Grundy.

Dunford, J.E. (1998) *Her Majesty's Inspectorate of Schools since 1944*. London: Woburn Press.

Gordon, P. (1988) 'Katharine Bathurst: a controversial woman inspector'. *History of Education*, 17(3), 193–207.

Gordon, P., Aldrich, R. and Dean, D. (1991) *Education and Policy In England in the Twentieth Century*. London: Woburn Press.

Gosden, P.H.J.H. (1976) *Education in the Second World War*. London: Methuen.

Lawton, D. and Gordon, P. (1987) *HMI*. London: Routledge and Kegan Paul.

Maclure, S. (1990) *A History of Education in London, 1870–1990*. London: Allen Lane.

— (2000) *The Inspectors' Calling. HMI and the shaping of educational policy, 1945–92*. London: Hodder and Stoughton.

Rhodes, G. (1981) *Inspectorates in British Government*. London: Allen and Unwin.

Savage, G.L. (1983) 'Social class and social policy: the civil service and secondary education in England during the interwar period'. *Journal of Contemporary History*, 18(2), 261–80.

Sherington, G. (1981) *English Education, Social Change and War, 1911–1920*. Manchester: Manchester University Press.

6 The 'liberal hour'? The Wilson government, race relations, immigrant youth and education, 1965–8

Dennis Dean

Richard Aldrich has been one of the vital practitioners whose work will enable historians of education to ensure that contemporary issues continue to be examined in historical and current contexts. As politicians now ignore education at their peril, we, as historians of education, can place our subject at the centre of historical debates about identity, social mobility, gender, ethnicity and economic and cultural changes.

Contemporary commentators (e.g. Rose 1969) portrayed the period from late 1965 until early 1968 as the 'liberal hour', signifying changes in the direction of race relations. Why had this situation happened? Much was attributed to Roy Jenkins's appointment at the Home Office to replace the more cautious, legalistic, Frank Soskice. Labour's substantial victory at the polls in March 1966 meant that they no longer had a wafer-thin majority and the tensions over race relations that had haunted the 1964 election had now eased. Personal factors and electoral fortune clearly played their part in shifting government policy.

Concern had mounted steadily from the late 1940s, when large numbers of West Indians began to arrive in Britain. Governments, both

Conservative and Labour, were forced by vociferous backbenchers, white pressure groups or media coverage to arrest rising anxieties about this. What issues dominated this early debate? Almost all the language focused on the need for regulation and control of immigration. Sharp divisions emerged within both governing parties about the necessity of controls, how they were to be administered and fears that clumsy regulation might damage relations with newly decolonised areas. Even after the passage of the 1962 Commonwealth Immigrants Act, these issues remained unresolved. Further disagreements continued over the extent of settlers' evasion and deceit, leading to a tightening of legislation in the shape of the Labour government's (first) 1965 Race Relations Act.

From the early 1960s, influenced by studies undertaken by the Race Relations Institute, attention turned from regulation to settlement and community relations, which, in turn, had repercussions for schooling. Other concerns arose about these new settlers' relationships to older communities and how this might affect the workplace, housing and the school playground. Did the new generation of West Indian or Asian children, growing up with their white counterparts, have different aspirations and ambitions to their parents? Would they be content to remain constricted in employment opportunities or training schemes when they left school? Was time changing perceptions? Anthony Lester, Roy Jenkins's adviser, argued that early immigrants 'were prepared to put up with a certain amount of indignity in exchange for employment and a higher standard of living. Their children born and educated here have made no similar commitment' (Lester to Maurice Foley, Under-Secretary of State for Economic Affairs, 6 May 1966, HO 376/158, National Archives [NA]). Government in the 1950s made certain assumptions: West Indian immigration was regarded as temporary, a consequence of the recent war that disturbed life patterns and unsettled populations all over the world. Once peacetime conditions returned, normality would resume, ex-servicemen would settle down and post-war reconstruction would be satisfied. Furthermore, it was widely thought that the Caribbean had always contained a mobile male population, apt to travel without their families to take advantage of employment prospects elsewhere. Many had wartime experience of Britain and news spread quickly of unfilled job vacancies there. Schools in the islands affirmed that they would be welcomed in the 'mother country', already insisting that it was now the heart of a multiracial Commonwealth.

Early commentators on West Indian life assumed that Christian, English-speaking immigrants would wish to assimilate and become black Britons, and that they would require an appreciation of the British sense of privacy and domesticity. Claims were made that West Indian males congregated in lodging houses and dance halls, where they attracted young white girls searching for exoticism and excitement. This was deemed dangerous because sexual competition created disorder. Churches, philanthropic societies and friendship councils, set up in areas of concentrated settlement, were seen as the proper agencies to undertake socialisation and accommodation.

Where West Indian families settled permanently, children were expected to attend neighbourhood schools and mix freely with their peer group. Even after clashes in Notting Hill and Nottingham, it was officially insisted 'that colour feeling is absent among schoolchildren and that relations between white and coloured people are quite natural and friendly' and that Education ministers 'feel that it would be a mistake to treat colour consciousness as a problem in our schools' (memorandum, 31 October 1961, HO 344/62, NA). But a joint parliamentary deputation had already raised doubts about these optimistic assessments that 'there was no problem in the schools' (notes of a deputation to R.A. Butler, Home Secretary, 22 July 1959, HO 344/42, NA). Butler was not persuaded by calls for the schools to explain why immigrants had entered the UK, pleading that 'the Minister of Education . . . has to be very careful about any action that might be considered as an attempt to influence the curriculum of such establishments' (Butler to Nigel Fisher MP, 3 November 1959, HO 344/42, NA). When problems arose, West Indian parents were blamed for not understanding that English schools were changing and that school discipline was becoming more relaxed. A police report, anticipating emotional stress among West Indian youth, commented 'West Indian parents seem to be strict with their children and adopt a Victorian attitude that they should be seen, not heard' (report by Superintendent Rose, 20 February 1964, HO 344/258, NA). Time was seen as necessary before full assimilation occurred.

Post-war British society was an unwelcoming place for newcomers. A long tradition of 'strangers in their midst' had been fanned by two long world wars with their stories of fifth columns and spies. Furthermore, a particular narrative about Britain's finest hour promoted complacency and a belief in British exceptionalism. While European neighbours suffered total defeat and upheaval, the perception was that Britain, through unity, coherence and the strength of its institutions, had destroyed the evil forces of totalitarianism. Its people now deserved their rewards in the form of a welfare state, improved health services and wider educational opportunities. Outsiders exploiting gains earned by wartime sacrifice could threaten all this. Furthermore, many servicemen had served in areas where white colonists were firmly entrenched and they returned, in peacetime, with a 'settler mentality'. The closing stages of decolonisation in the Middle East, Cyprus and particularly Kenya in the Mau Mau uprising of the early 1950s, strengthened these prejudices. Assimilation was not easily acceptable to groups influenced by these considerations.

From the mid-1950s new waves of immigrants arrived from the Indian subcontinent. Unlike West Indians, they were seen as less boisterous, willing to keep themselves to themselves and unlikely to become involved with the wider community. However, they presented other difficulties since they differed in dress and religion, and often did not possess basic English skills. Government circles expressed concern at the growth of an impenetrable, alien culture, defensive in nature and resistant to British education: 'The one point that stands out is that as far as assimilation is concerned the Indians might as well be creatures from another planet' (memorandum, 21 April 1962, HO 344/194, NA). These new arrivals, together with stories of frequent clashes between West Indian and white youths, challenged early complacent views of race relations. Schools as the melting pot, or time as a reconciler, were no longer thought to hold the key to solving current difficulties.

The emergence of sociology, the revitalisation of social history and early forays into cultural studies heightened the profile of community relations generally (e.g. Hoggart 1957; Young and Wilmot 1957; Thompson 1961). Displacement of well-established neighbourhoods, together with social mobility, new service industries and increased educational opportunities, raised fresh problems. What happened to those stranded in this era of change? West Indians and Asians were caught up in this debate. They were viewed as one constituent of twilight areas defined by poor housing, welfare facilities and schools.

A growing anxiety centred around the young. A chasm seemed to open up with the older generation conditioned by the Depression, war and post-war austerity. Mass communication, American influence and affluence each influenced the ambitions and lifestyles of young people, but there was also a deep unease about the future. Decline pervaded contemporary commentaries, fanned by unfavourable comparisons with European competitors. All this came in the closing stages of decolonisation, a retreat of British influence on the world stage and sexual scandals rocking the political establishment. Why had Britain apparently fallen behind? A populist view searching for scapegoats concentrated on outsiders, destroying what was seen as a once unified, homogenous national community. This malaise could be stemmed by strict immigration control.

The Conservative government's 1962 Commonwealth Immigrants Act was passed, despite strong opposition. Immigrant numbers continued to rise, however, leading to calls to investigate the possible fraudulent evasion of the legislation. A government crisis ensued: few Conservative ministers wished to separate families, seen as the source of stable society, but, on the other hand, the presence of a new supply of wives and children, arriving to join their husbands and fathers, increased numbers. Paradoxically, the 1961 Act, perhaps more than any other factor, established settlements in the UK (Spencer 1997: 129–30).

Early in the 1960s, certain local education authorities (LEAs) concentrated attention on new entrants arriving during the school term. How were these new pupils, with little English, to be fitted to their new surroundings? How much separate introductory teaching was required and where should it initially take place? What new teaching materials and training programmes for teachers were required? Through the teaching of the new language it was hoped that this young generation would become accustomed to their surroundings. It was hoped that this would facilitate breakthroughs into communities that were firmly establishing their own environments and assuage the worry that self-contained 'ghettos' were appearing in some inner-city areas.

In 1964 a new Labour government, led by Harold Wilson, gave warning of a new approach, leading officials at the new Department of Education and Science (DES) to anticipate the necessity 'of giving some kind of advice to authorities' (memorandum, 5 November 1964, ED 147/594, NA). Wilson has been criticised for failing to capitalise on this mood and concentrating too much on holding power and forming political compromises, but the travails of later prime ministers and publication of Bernard Donoughue's diaries (2005) have led to kinder reassessments of Wilson. In terms of race relations, as he recalled in his first volume of memoirs, Wilson faced a divided Cabinet and party, anxious about the numbers of immigrants arriving in Britain through the widespread evasion of statutory controls (Wilson 1971: 121). His initial instinct was to restrict numbers, but he also needed to satisfy MPs who demanded measures to end racial discrimination and to promote better community relations. His twin policies, which were always at odds with each other, therefore, were to strictly control immigrant numbers while promoting integration. This prompted the National Committee for Commonwealth Immigrants (NCCI) to warn 'that the Home Secretary should be made aware of the dangers of immigrant control to the world of community relations' (note by Frank Cousins, Chairman, Race Relations Board, January 1969, CK 3/713, NA).

Despite these criticisms, Wilson had raised issues that were to be pursued by more progressive politicians and pressure groups. How far should the law be used to challenge acts of discrimination and should it be applied more widely to cover housing and employment? Was coercion or education, or a mixture, to be the course pursued? In tackling these issues, Roy Jenkins at the Home Office became the key figure. He had been heavily involved in the Labour Party's 1950s 'revisionist' controversy, aimed at making Labour less a party of class, shrouded in austerity and regulation, and more in tune with modern times. This entailed finding a more progressive programme likely to appeal to more affluent, better-educated sections of the community. In this context, the party needed to scrap restrictive laws and traditions and find policies allowing individuals to develop their own capabilities. Jenkins favoured the relaxation of censorship, reform of divorce laws and the decriminalisation of homosexuality. He regarded the 1965 Race Relations Act, at its worst, as shoddy, and, at best, as an instrument needing revision. To improve community relations, terms like 'assimilation' and 'accommodation' that overemphasised incoming groups and placed too little onus on existing society were to be discarded. He supported the contention that 'the Scots, Irish, Welsh have maintained separate identities, while being integrated into British society. The same must be achieved by West Indians, Pakistanis, Indians' (Lester to Foley, 6 May 1966, HO 376/158, NA).

How much did Jenkins collaborate with fellow revisionist Tony Crosland, the Secretary of State for Education? Their priorities were not identical. Crosland's concern was to extend educational opportunity to wider sections of the population stunted by early selection and a narrowly meritocratic system, heavily weighted in favour of well-entrenched groups. Only with the reorganisation of secondary education, to be followed by a review of higher education, could this be attained. This would ultimately benefit all communities since, he told the 1966 North of England Education Conference, 'I believe this represents a strong and unstoppable pressure in British society to extend the rights of citizenship' (quoted in Leonard 1974: 194). Junior ministers and departmental officials were left to deal with what Crosland saw as ancillary issues like dispersion.

Jenkins's hopes for a swift widening of race relations legislation to include employment and housing, following the 1966 election, proved more difficult. Ray Gunter, Minister of Labour, supported by trades unions and employers, mounted strong resistance to what was seen as government interference in industrial relations. He maintained that 'this problem is not going to be solved by exhortations by national bodies' (Gunter to Alice Bacon, Education Minister, [n.d.] 1966, HO 376/106, NA). Many continued to argue that the principal impediments to black workers' employment and promotion resulted not from discrimination but from 'the immigrant's ability and lack of sufficiently high educational standard' (E. Thornton, Parliamentary Secretary, Ministry of Labour to Foley, 18 June 1965, LAB 43/433, NA). These sentiments needed time to be broken.

Jenkins used a number of instruments. The appointment of a close associate to chair the Race Relations Board signalled that existing legislation was too limited. Not only did Mark Bonham Carter have direct access to Jenkins, he also confronted the pretence 'that neither immigration nor race relations gave rise to serious problems and that, if they did these problems will disappear with the passage of time, weathered by the tolerant attitude we live in' (Bonham Carter 1970: 4). For his part, Jenkins toured various educational and regional conferences spelling out his vision of good community relations. He and his advisers maintained continual contact with a range of agencies, employing university-trained researchers from the Institute of Race Relations, the newly formed Runnymede Trust and the established group known as Political and Economic Planning (PEP). Lessons were drawn from the USA and, particularly, from the writings of Gunnar Myrdal who argued that 'in the United States the Negro problem was in reality the white man's problem and . . . it was white men's behaviour towards the Negro that had created and perpetuated the problem' (Rose 1969: 4). What was urgently required was a magisterial British study, like Mydral's, that exposed discrimination and prejudice suffered by Asians and West Indians in their search for employment, housing and educational opportunities. Jenkins carefully avoided a government inquiry that would be accused of improper influence. Although privately financed, the 1967 PEP report on racial discrimination was both promoted and used by the Home Office and the Race Relations Board to reveal the extent of discrimination and to undermine Cabinet opposition. Equally important were tactics used by newly formed groups within the West Indian and Asian communities, drawing on strategies employed by the US Civil Rights campaigns to expose shortcomings in the existing legislation.

One factor that revealed the problems of new communities was the clamour that followed publication of the DES's Circular 7/65, *The Education of Immigrants*. This provoked discussion on two counts. The DES concluded that many Asian or West Indian children could no longer be classified as immigrants, since they had been born in the UK and had shared the educational experiences of their contemporaries. More contentiously, the department strayed into debates about high concentrations of certain ethnic groups in particular schools. The advice given was that each school ought to contain no more than 30 per cent of its pupils from the New Commonwealth. Thus, the debates over dispersion had changed their parameters.

The Conservative Edward Boyle had become deeply involved in all aspects of race relations while Education Minister in the early 1960s. He expressed alarm at the situation in parts of the West Midlands, where he feared both the growth of ghettos and his own government's tolerance of them. White society, he claimed, wished to contain new communities in areas with their own shops, places of entertainment and schools. Boyle feared a drift into segregation and recommended that schools should challenge this by absorbing groups of Asian and West Indian students into their classrooms. He insisted, 'we ought as a party to stand for the principle of integration and not for the acceptance of de facto segregation' (memorandum by Boyle,

10 December 1962, CAB 134/1507, NA). LEAs in northern England and parts of London approached matters more pragmatically, and strategies were developed to disperse immigrant children more evenly across schools under their jurisdiction.

By 1965, the arguments for dispersal now included the necessity for younger generations to abandon the lifestyles of their parents. A new note had crept in, particularly after Peter Griffiths, a local headmaster, won the Smethwick constituency for the Conservatives in 1964. His appeal was directed to so-called 'beleaguered white groups', marooned in areas of high immigrant concentration. Unlike wealthier whites, they could not escape to more affluent suburbs and, as a result, a generation of white children was allegedly 'trapped' in schools where their needs were neglected and they risked being absorbed into an alien culture.

Despite a defence by Denis Howell, a junior Education minister and Birmingham MP, Circular 7/65 raised great anger among those who believed that dispersion threatened to destroy collaboration between parents and neighbourhood schools. Little evidence was produced to suggest that such a programme would lead to dramatic improvements in language teaching for pupils unused to English. Howell conceded that 'the parent who took their children away from schools where there was a high proportion of immigrants did so on educational rather than on racial grounds' (note by Howell, 21 December 1965, ED 147/594, NA), though in many instances this seems doubtful. The net effect was to condemn schools with a high immigrant concentration as defective. There were liberal critics of dispersion, too. For them, concentrations of West Indian and Asian populations resulted from discrimination which restricted them to poor housing and menial employment. This needed to be broken: 'Problems of dispersal can only be solved by positive action to desegregate housing' (note by Tony Smyth, Chairman, National Council for Civil Liberties, 24 September 1965, ED 147/594, NA).

As concerns about community relations replaced immigration control on the political agenda, attention shifted to reappraisals of disadvantage and deprivation and reconsideration of post-war welfare provision. Shortcomings were exposed and opinions divided over new questions. Did these communities share in the problems of ill-defined but significant underclasses, or did they require special treatment because of the colour of their skin and their origins? In relation to schooling, the Plowden Report (DES 1967) recommended the designation of educational priority areas to offset high staff turnover, depressing school surroundings and inadequate resources and buildings. Special funds were set aside and research projects established, but the trap of targeting particular groups was avoided. Lady Plowden's Committee struggled over the question of immigrant children: 'Some of their needs are very similar to those of children in educational priority areas; others are not' (DES 1967: 69).

The late 1960s was dominated by images of racial disturbances in many US cities, shown regularly on British television. Questions surfaced about their implications for British society. Jenkins and his supporters insisted that comparisons were not easily made. Discrimination was more widely practised in the USA, the black population was more extensive and suffered from the burdens of slavery. Yet lessons needed to be absorbed. First of all, necessary reforms had been delayed and the consequences were that the more moderate, gradualist leadership lost followers to more militant groups. If this was to be avoided in Britain, reform and changes in attitude must be speedily embarked upon. Second, just as the law had been used in both the USA and South Africa to bolster segregation and oppression, it must now be used to set boundaries on unreasonable behaviour. This was happening in the USA, but too late.

The focus turned increasingly to young people in the new communities, many of them educated in Britain. Were they being seduced by more militant figures into acts of defiance? More pragmatically, how did they spend their leisure time? The spotlight fell on youth services and their success in attracting adolescents. It was evident that many voluntary organisations involved in the provision of services failed to attract West Indian or Asian youngsters. If they were drawn at all into the ambit of youth and sporting clubs, neither Asians nor West Indians were likely to stray from their own communities. The Hunt Committee, set up to investigate the issue in 1966, was sharply divided on how to make progress. One group supported the view that it was preferable that young people were in clubs, even if they were segregated. This could be temporary because 'it was possible to regard immigrant children [as being] at an interim stage in the process of integration leading into the easier assimilation of young immigrants into the mainstream of youth activities at a later period' ('Committee on Immigrant and Youth Services', 16 February 1966, ED 147/523, NA). It was felt that segregated clubs could be associated with wider civic federations collaborating in youth activities. Other members were more pessimistic: too many educational expedients had been promoted as temporary measures to be discarded once situations had settled down. Indeed, this was precisely Howell's argument when addressing angry protest deputations over his support for dispersal. Stuart Hall reflected ruefully, 'Structures which are set up for transitional purposes especially in England and notably in education, have a very nasty habit of becoming permanent establishments which people spend a lifetime trying to dismantle' (memorandum, [n.d.] 1966, ED 147/523, NA).

Of increasing significance from the late 1960s was a pressure group, drawn particularly from the West Indian community, which scrutinised more critically what was provided for their children. Teachers' assumptions about West Indian schoolchildren's shortcomings were questioned, most persuasively in Bernard Coard's (1971) *How the West Indian Child is made Educationally Subnormal in the British School System*. These views brought a response from those engaged in race relations research. In a study of the Birmingham suburb of Sparkbrook, Rex and Moore highlighted cultural gaps between classroom teachers and West Indian pupils: 'The teachers see their role as putting over a certain set of values (Christian), a code of behaviour (middle class) and a set of academic and job aspirations in which white collar jobs have a higher prestige than manual, clean jobs rather than dirty' (Rex and Moore 1967: 237). Even the DES began to respond, accepting that 'Perhaps the most controversial form of arrangements is the one whereby immigrant children are regarded as within the province of a local authority or school remedial service' (DES 1971: 37). Pressure groups from within were ultimately successful in exposing a 'hidden curriculum' that presented, in textbooks and written materials, or by the manner of teachers, powerful images of white superiority or black inferiority. But this success was only partial and did not lessen the numbers of West Indian pupils being labelled as 'backward'.

Debates about decline, together with the success of European competitors, inevitably raised concerns about the training of the labour force, its inability to adapt to changing patterns and the failings of British industry to cope with new technology. For example, what happened to highly qualified recent Asian arrivals who discovered that employers avoided their use in supervisory positions, and denied access to promotion and extended training? After visiting areas of high Commonwealth settlement, Foley was disturbed 'that for various reasons a number of immigrants who were quite capable of doing skilled and professional work, are, in fact, engaged in unskilled work' (Foley to Thornton, 28 April 1965, LAB 43/433, NA). This issue affected teaching appointments, particularly in a period when schools suffered from an acute shortage of trained teachers. Complaints reached the director of education for Wolverhampton that Indian and Pakistani graduates were being employed as bus conductors rather than being absorbed as teachers. His response was robust and unsympathetic: 'On interview the great majority are found to be so deficient in English speech that they are incomprehensible to me and my officials and could not possibly communicate with children.' He continued, 'with only very few exceptions the few we have employed here failed in teaching techniques and are a burden to the staff in this respect' (letter to H. Leadbitter, 15 March 1968, HLG 118/778, NA). He feared that the introduction of a new Race Relations Act might see him faced with charges of discrimination. In the final stages of that legislation, government departments, including Education, besieged the Home Office for special treatment from the Race Relations Board. LEAs that dispersed high concentrations of Asian or West Indian pupils on educational grounds supported their demands. Hackney's Director of Education argued 'that some authorities sought to disperse their coloured intakes and this could be regarded as discriminatory when the intention was to help integration'. He supported the assertion 'that as the problem of race relations was essentially one of education the Board should have a special relationship with the Ministry of Education and Science' (letter, 15 March 1968, HLG 118/778, NA).

The 'liberal hour' assumed that immigration controls, introduced by Wilson in 1965, had effectively quietened concerns about continuous streams, particularly from the Asian subcontinent, arriving in the UK. This enabled Jenkins to develop the second track, the promotion of a community relations programme that would effectively deal with discriminatory practices. Within the Home Office, anxieties always remained about the implication of concessions, agreed by Iain Macleod, in negotiations leading to Kenyan independence back in 1956. These had conceded that large sections of the Asian population in that area could be granted British passports, which meant they were not subject to immigration controls. In 1967 the Kenyan government decided on a policy of 'Africanisation', determining that Asians who had retained British citizenship were displaced from their positions. Many decided to leave Kenya for the UK and Duncan Sandys, an ex-Commonwealth Secretary, demanded that the flow be stopped. Pressure rose from particular areas, notably Wolverhampton, that local services, especially the schools, were already overwhelmed.

Anxieties about absorptive capacities resurfaced. Attempts to persuade the Kenyan government to reconsider its policies failed, despite Wilson's plea to Daniel Moi that the absorption of immigrants into British society 'would cause difficulties if it was done too quickly', prejudicing community and race relations and the well-being of existing immigrants (Wilson to Moi, [n.d.] 1968, PREM 3/3743, NA). The upshot was the Commonwealth Immigrants Act of March 1968. Any citizen of the UK or colonies who was the holder of a British passport would now be subject to immigration control unless they or a parent or grandparent had been born or naturalised in Britain. This effectively rendered Kenyan Asians as stateless.

The measure caused political storms. Labour dynasties divided: David Ennals, the Home Office Minister, defended the legislation, while his brother Martin became a spokesman for stateless East African Asians. From the back benches, Tom Driberg expressed alarm about government policy and linked it with other disagreements: 'On this, as on other subjects, a certain amount of embarrassment and inconvenience can be explained when the policies of government and party differ from each other' (letter, 13 February 1968, HO 344/197, NA). On the Conservative side, allies of Macleod expressed anger that support from the Opposition front bench blatantly disregarded assurances once given by their own government. The legislation, coinciding with hesitancy over sanctions in Rhodesia, did little to strengthen Wilson's efforts to build close relationships with the new Commonwealth countries. Disillusion spread both ways: there was anger that India, Pakistan and other Commonwealth nations had done little to aid British efforts to ease the predicament.

The legislation brought angry reactions not only within the Asian community but also among Jenkins's allies in the academic world. Nicholas Deakin withdrew as an adviser, while the NCCI, presided over by Archbishop Michael Ramsey, expressed outrage that it had not even been consulted about the implications of the rushed measure. This organisation, set up in 1965, was intended to organise a network of professional agents in the localities to foster community relations. Many of its members, notably Richard Tittmus, agreed to serve only if they were free to criticise government actions, especially on immigration issues. Even with a sympathetic Jenkins, the NCCI pursued an independent line and clashed with government departments including Education, which was prone to interfere with their procedures.

It was a new home secretary, James Callaghan, who steered the 1968 Commonwealth Immigrants Act through. He combated internal

Cabinet dissension, particularly from the newly reorganised Foreign and Commonwealth Office, which was concerned about damage to Britain's moral standing among non-aligned nations. Other dissenters, such as George Thomas, argued that East African Asians ought to be given exceptional treatment. They were accustomed to the English language from an early age and possessed professional, entrepreneurial and supervisory skills that could be exploited in the British economy. Callaghan acted on realism. He explained, 'the opposition it seems to me are likely to become more extreme about immigration questions as the election draws near' (Callaghan to Wilson, 18 February 1969, HO 344/197, NA). He ignored protests from the Cabinet, the Labour Party and outside bodies and, using as a pretext Ramsey's wish to resign from the large and unwieldy NCCI, he replaced it with the smaller, and he hoped more amenable, Community Relations Commission. Ominous changes were in the air: the Joint Council for the Welfare of Immigrants was established, mainly as a response to the formation, in 1967, of the anti-immigrant National Front.

Jenkins was clearly disturbed at the change in atmosphere throughout 1968. Callaghan, who maintained close relations with the Police Federation while an Opposition frontbencher, bowed to pressure from this organisation and conceded that racial discrimination was not to be a specific offence against the police. Jenkins protested that complaints were constantly being made of police harassment, particularly of West Indian teenagers.

> After a year in which the government has been compelled to force through the Kenyan Immigrants Bill and began to talk (quite rightly) to the Smith regime on a basis unacceptable to many of our supporters inside and outside Parliament a decision on the Police's proposal by the Home Secretary would cause deep resentment.
>
> (Jenkins to Wilson, 11 November 1968, PREM 13/2883, NA)

The perception of the second Labour Race Relations Act (1968) was not as Jenkins would have wished. It had been highlighted as the cornerstone of a programme that would determine the framework of good community relations and public education, and be a signal to end discrimination. Instead, it became seen as a quid pro quo for squalid, rushed legislation, caused by panic. At best, it was regarded as a safety mechanism to fend off critics at home and abroad who were quick to blame the government for bending to racial intolerance.

While local politicians and pressure groups tempted the Conservative Opposition to emphasise immigration issues, no major political figure endorsed this strategy. Enoch Powell changed this situation in 1968, leading Alan Watkins to warn that 'he is now in fact the most dangerous type of demagogue' (Watkins 1968: 534). Powell's words reflected an educated voice of protest. The people themselves had never been consulted about integration, immigration, race relations and the introduction of anti-discrimination laws. Policy had been agreed by a coterie of ministers aided by elite public opinion that had little real knowledge of the impact of immigration. Too much attention was paid either to leaders of the New Commonwealth or to world opinion, mainly to keep up illusions about Britain's position in the world. Britain must stand on its own feet. A spurious Commonwealth bore no relation to the old Empire that had shaped Britain's character. Finally, before it was too late, it was vital to rescue an English identity and restore English traditions, heritage and history in the classroom. The alternative path – steady progress towards a multicultural society – threatened to undermine past strengths in British society. Subsequent support for Powell's stance, particularly in working-class areas, struck fear within government. Burke Trend, the Cabinet Secretary, urged ministers to visit trouble spots 'to ensure the understanding of the extent of the control of immigration and the Government's determination to improve conditions in congested areas'. It was also agreed 'that particular attention should be paid to improving educational facilities' (briefing note by Trend, 15 May 1968, PREM 13/2883, NA).

The common picture that has emerged of the 1960s has been of a permissive, iconoclastic and challenging era. Furthermore, it has been viewed as the basis for a reform impetus that has continued fitfully even into this century. Legislation like the Race Relations Acts and such organisations as the Commission for Racial Equality steadily extended their powers. Various strategies have been promoted to end discrimination and the educational world has been heavily involved in these undertakings. Changes have been instigated to deal with curriculum, resources and teacher training to meet the needs of an ever-changing multicultural society. But whereas Jenkins had anticipated that once sources of discrimination had been diagnosed by an army of new professionals and academics these people would then direct and support local civic and religious leaders in the drive to overturn obstacles to improve community relations, localism has been on the retreat.

Nevertheless, this 1960s legacy was always a contested one. Powell graphically represented the views of those who felt they were being ignored or supplanted. He devoted his attention to the dangers of further decline and loss of identity, which he ascribed to the numerous decisions taken by the political elite in the 1960s. These themes were to be repeated during the Thatcher era and vitally affected the way in which successive waves of incomers have been regarded. In turn, the educational world has often been attacked for collusion in undermining a stable society. In the future, our educational experience is likely to operate in a world where local economic conditions in many parts of the globe, together with rapid population growth and further developments in mass communications and transportation, will stimulate more waves of migration to areas where labour is in demand. The issues raised in the 1960s, consequently, are not likely to go away and need to be examined in depth and with perspective.

References

Bonham Carter, M. (1970) *Migration and Race* (Earl Grey Memorial Lecture). Newcastle: University of Newcastle.

Coard, B. (1971) *How the West Indian Child is made Educationally Subnormal in the British School System: The scandal of the black child in schools in Britain.* London: New Beacon for the Caribbean Education and Community Workers' Association.

Department of Education and Science (DES) (1967) *Children and Their Primary Schools* (Plowden Report). Volume I. London: HMSO.
— (1971) *The Education of Immigrants* (Education Survey 13). London: HMSO.
Donoughue, B. (2005) *Downing Street Diary: With Harold Wilson in No. 10.* London: Jonathan Cape.
Hoggart, R. (1957) *The Uses of Literacy: Aspects of working-class life with special reference to publications and entertainments.* Harmondsworth: Penguin.
Leonard, D. (ed.) (1974) *Socialism Now, And Other Essays by Anthony Crosland.* London: Cape.
Rex, J. and Moore, R. (1967) *Race, Community, and Conflict: A study of Sparkbrook.* Oxford: Oxford University Press.
Rose, E.J.B. (ed.) (1969) *Colour and Citizenship: A report on British race relations.* Oxford: Oxford University Press.
Spencer, I.R.G. (1997) *British Immigration Policy since 1939: The making of multi-racial Britain.* London: Routledge.
Thompson, E.P. (1961) *The Making of the English Working Class.* London: Gollancz.
Watkins, A. (1968) 'Enoch and after'. *New Statesman,* 75, 11 May: 534.
Wilson, H. (1971) *The Labour Government, 1964–1970: A personal record.* London: Weidenfeld and Nicolson.
Young, M. and Wilmot, P. (1957) *Family and Kinship in East London.* London: Routledge and Kegan Paul.

7 Who decides what children learn and how they should learn it? The recent historical experience of the United Kingdom

Roy Lowe

Introduction

The work of historians of education sometimes involves posing basic questions about the nature and workings of modern society. Much of the work initiated and conducted by Richard Aldrich has involved asking fundamental questions about the recent development of schooling, and demonstrating the significance of educational change for social development. In the introduction to *Education for the Nation*, he stressed that his 'substantial purpose' was to 'provide a basis for the restoration of informed discussion and decision-making in education . . . to increase the understanding of education in this country' (Aldrich 1996: 2). This chapter in Richard's honour is written in that spirit and towards that end.

Richard Aldrich's work stands alongside that of Brian Simon, who in a lengthy career raised the possibility that popular education, as provided by the State, was not popular at all but in reality represented an attempt by those in power to establish through schooling a form of social control which ensured the ongoing separation of social groups and social classes (Simon 1960, 1965, 1974, 1991). Similarly, Fritz

Ringer's work (1979) identified schooling as a device whose key function was to impose forms of social stratification right across the industrialising world. Although Ringer's work focuses on north-west Europe during the period of industrialisation, it has implications for current developments in countries such as China and India. Many historians have focused on gender issues, and in particular on the ways in which schools and higher education have been devices for the establishment and maintenance of distinctions between the sexes and for the promotion of different social routes and lifestyles for boys and girls (e.g. contributors to Lowe 2000, vol. 1, part V). Each of these debates impinges on, and needs to be kept in mind, whilst approaching the issues in this chapter.

In two recent public statements (Lowe 2002, 2005), I have argued for a new history of education which addresses the pressing issues confronting humankind at the present time, in particular global warming and the stark contrasts between rich and poor countries. It is time for historians to focus on, and go some way to explain, the role of schooling in establishing and maintaining these contrasts. Whilst the present chapter falls short of these major issues, it does address what must surely be seen as a central question for all educators. What should children be taught in schools and who should be making the decisions? How should they learn it? Another question necessarily arises, too: should all children be taught the same things or are differing curricula and teaching methods preferable for different groups of children? These questions are of significance not just for historians, but for all involved in education. The chapter argument will be founded in historical research but will necessarily involve some speculation and some claims which go beyond that narrow brief. Issues are raised which no one individual can hope to answer fully, but which none the less demand a response from anyone involved in the act of 'educating' children.

Two strands in the debate on schooling

Since the coming of popular education it has been possible to identify those who would set strict limits on what should constitute an education (particularly that of the common people) and those who held more lofty ambitions. Bernard de Mandeville in the eighteenth century, Bell, Lancaster, Davies Giddy and Bishop Fraser of Manchester in the nineteenth, each, in their own way, held to a very limited view of what was possible in school. Their pronouncements are well known and stand as an indictment of many who, through popular schooling, sought to keep the lower orders in their proper place (see Sylvester 1970: 176–82, 286–7; Simon 1960: 132; Maclure 1965: 79–80).

Their views have been echoed in some of the arguments of the emerging radical right in the period since the Second World War. Geoffrey Bantock, Professor of Education at the University of Leicester, argued publicly, in 1961, that

> syllabuses can only be built up as a result of honest admission of radical differences of ability. . . . We seem to be committed to the attempt, doomed to failure from the start, to bring all elements of the population to a similar level of consciousness. . . . In the school for the average child, the domestic life will concern the girls . . . for the boys an interest in the machine will play a major part. . . . What goes out? Formal history and geography should disappear. . . . Much waste matter could be removed from the mathematics syllabus. No second language should be studied. . . . What a school CAN accomplish is always sadly limited.
>
> (*The Times Educational Supplement*, 6 January 1961: 11)

The grounds on which such arguments were based may have changed beyond recognition, particularly given the input of the growing army of professional psychometricians during the twentieth century, but the central claim, that the education of the majority must remain strictly limited, appears remarkably familiar. In 1980, Roger Scruton observed that

> the attempt to provide equality of opportunity . . . is simply a confused stumble in the dark. . . . It is simply not possible to provide universal

> education. Nor, indeed, is it desirable. . . . The appetite for learning
> points people in only a certain direction: it siphons them away from
> those places where they might have been contented.
>
> (Scruton 1980: 75)

The determination to set limits on the schooling of the bulk of the population has been evident more recently in claims for the primacy of the so-called 'core curriculum'. Thatcherite and post-Thatcherite arguments that schooling must be 'useful' in terms of its relationship to employment and must be shown through inspection and public accounting to be both effective and efficient all bear marks of this nineteenth-century legacy.

This observation is equally true of the second major strand in educational discourse, namely the appeal to the nature, the needs and the interests of the child. Set against the arguments that the extent of education should be strictly limited, there have, for over two centuries, been those who took a radically different view of the potential of humankind. The high priests of this movement are also extremely familiar to us. Jean-Jacques Rousseau, starting from what was seen at the time as the extremely controversial proposition that 'there is no original sin' in the human heart, spelt out an educational regime which was essentially libertarian and heuristic. Based on an attempt to explain the nature of childhood and to devise the educational regime which best suited that, Rousseau told the teacher:

> it is rarely your business to suggest what he ought to learn. . . . You
> should put it within his reach, should skilfully awaken the desire and
> supply him with the means for its satisfaction. . . . Let all the lessons of
> young people take the form of doing rather than talking; let them
> learn nothing from books that they can learn from experience.
>
> (Rousseau 1911: 142, 214)

These ideas, linked to the Pestalozzian view that all education was derived from sense impressions, became the basis of Robert Owen's claims that all humankind were rational beings and that it was the responsibility of the educator to 'either give the poor a rational or useful training, or mock not their ignorance, their poverty and their misery by merely instructing them to become conscious of the degradation under which they exist' (Silver 1965: 108). This underlying theme of the improvability of humankind underpinned the thinking of all those who pressed the claims of so-called 'progressive' education through the nineteenth and twentieth centuries. A host of figures such as Maria Montessori and Homer Lane, as well as those involved in the turn-of-the-century child-study movement, took a radically different view of both human potential and of educational methods from those who would set strict limits to what was possible in the classroom.

This became very evident in the period immediately following the Second World War. Advocates of child-centred education, of the 'play way' and of discovery methods seemed, briefly at least, to be in control of the rhetoric around popular education. John Newsom, the chief education officer of Hertfordshire, believed 'that the child was educated by the whole environment in which he or she was taught . . . he wanted schools that elevated the spirit and ennobled the mind' (Maclure 1984: 37–60). Newsom, with Alec Clegg in the West Riding and Stewart Mason in Leicestershire, were among the leading administrators advocating a progressive approach at this time.

The popularity of these ideas extended beyond teacher educators and primary school specialists. Indeed, *The New Secondary Education* reported the official government view that

> the majority of children learn most easily by dealing with things following a course rooted in their own day-to-day experience. . . . The majority will do best . . . in an atmosphere which enables them to develop freely along their own lines.
>
> (Ministry of Education 1947: 22–3)

The influence of this lobby was so powerful that, in the years following 1945, child-centred education, the 'play way', activity methods, destreaming and the use of projects became almost universal rallying cries within education and were widely promulgated to the growing army of teacher training students.

Thus, for over two centuries, it has been possible to discern two conflicting themes in the debate on schooling: the one limiting, hierarchical and involving exclusivity; the other more open, underpinned by a view of the shared qualities of humankind rather than what differentiates them, and more ready to place responsibility on the shoulders of the learner. What can we learn from this dichotomy? What can it tell us about the central questions of what children should be taught, how they should be taught and who should decide on these issues?

The curriculum: what should children be taught?

It is not oversimplifying to claim that the origins of popular schooling during the early industrial revolution were driven by several interlinked motives. Acceptance of the national religion, obedience, the training of a docile and cooperative labour force which was not overeducated and (particularly in view of events in France) the avoidance of revolution: these were the main concerns. All of this was brilliantly summarised by Richard Johnson (1970) as the imposition of social control. He saw the introduction of the schools' Inspectorate in the 1840s as the visible token of the imposition of that control, which remains important today. Any society that publicly funds an activity such as teaching understandably seeks to maintain some degree of control over how those monies are spent. Recently, in the United States of America, for example, the teaching of evolution has been banned in several states (see *Guardian*, 25 October 2005: 17). A list of topics and themes that are either proscribed or discouraged in schools in different parts of the globe could quickly be compiled.

Two themes are especially apposite when we consider the school curriculum in industrial Britain. The first has to do with elite education. Not only did the 'establishment' seek to put strict limits on the education of the working poor, the need to devise an appropriate form of schooling for their own children also led to the development of a powerful system of nineteenth-century private schools in which the curriculum approach was entirely different. The 1864 Parliamentary Report on the public schools commented that it is not easy to estimate

> the degree to which the English people are indebted to these schools . . . or their capacity to govern others and control themselves . . . their aptitude for combining freedom with order. . . . These schools have been the chief nurseries of our statesmen. They have perhaps the largest share in moulding the character of an English gentleman.
>
> (Chandos 1984: 328)

This distinctiveness of the public schools was founded on a curriculum which wove the teaching of modern subjects around a core of classical studies and which depended also on particular approaches to curriculum and teaching so as to encourage qualities such as self-assurance, independence of mind and leadership, all of which were thought to be important for the future lives of the pupils and for the British Empire. In brief, a differing career route required a quite different school curriculum. It is interesting, and significant, too, that although these schools have become subject to inspection by the State, they remain largely outside and aloof from political debates on the school curriculum and they continue to thrive. They have educated roughly 7 per cent of the population throughout the period since the Second World War, and they continue to do so.

Second, it is clear that swift economic change, particularly the development of what is best described as the second industrial revolution at the end of the nineteenth century, led to a growing need for curriculum change. On the one hand, industrialists were determined that the schools should not become places where trade secrets were communicated to young people who might end up working for their rivals. But, at the same time, it was vital that a more highly trained and an essentially literate labour force was generated to staff the growing electrical, chemical and engineering businesses which were

very different from the earlier textile, mining and ironworking industries where a literate workforce would have been almost a distraction.
Thus, economic change has been another constant in the debate on
the school curriculum. Whether it is the white blouse revolution and
the rise of the female secretary during the Edwardian era, or the rise
of the service industries and the tertiary sector after the Second World
War, or the computer revolution and the globalisation of knowledge
most recently, whatever the impulse, there has been a succession of
new strands in the debate on the curriculum during the past 150 years.
These strands have always demanded that schools should offer their
pupils 'useful' experiences, though understandings of what was most
useful at any particular time changed.

Curriculum differentiation

If the distinction of the public schools from those of the common
people was underpinned by a belief that differing curricula were
needed for rich and poor, the evolving economic and social context
was to lead to its own dynamic of curriculum differentiation within
the fast-growing state sector. The rise of specialisation and of examinations supported the argument that some children would have to
follow different curricular routes from others. By the mid-nineteenth
century, this was becoming an element in public policy. The 1868
Schools Inquiry Commission, chaired by Henry Baron Taunton, assumed
that the expansion of secondary education would necessarily cater
separately for those whose parents wished them to stay in school to
18 years of age, those wishing to leave at 16 and those who saw no
need of an education beyond 14. This meant three grades of secondary
school with different curricula. Significantly, it was the parents whose
wishes were to be paramount. And, significantly, during the following
30 years, when over 1,000 secondary schools were reconstituted by the
Schools Commissioners appointed in 1869, although a major effort was
made to impose three differing curricula (classical, modern and basic

skills), with every school being designated first, second or third grade, in reality, teachers defeated the plan by simply adding those subjects which were not prescribed for their own school as additional subjects available after normal school hours at a fee. The distinctions became increasingly those of wealth and class, while curricula became increasingly similar across all schools of whatever type.

This proved to be almost an exact model for developments during the following century. A succession of government initiatives set out to impose different kinds of specialisation on the secondary schools. In the 1890s it was the higher grade schools set up to teach the sciences, while central schools were expected to prepare their pupils for particular kinds of employment in the early twentieth century. After the Second World War, new arguments (that children had differing kinds of mind and so needed different curricula) were advanced, but the attempt to distinguish between grammar, modern and technical schools bore all the hallmarks of the nineteenth-century planners. More recently, city technology colleges, specialist schools and academies have sought to differentiate curricula, with the interests and aspirations of the pupils ostensibly justifying the differentiation. Finally, in the autumn of 2005, the Labour government announced, in its twelfth Education White Paper, the introduction of 'self-governing' schools, which would enable parents to control a school's 'ethos and individualism' (DfES 2005). Over a century and a half the grounds have constantly shifted, but the central intention, to offer differing curricula to different pupils, has remained amazingly intact.

A few historical moments stand out as bucking this trend. The first was the publication of Robert Morant's 1904 *Regulations for Secondary Schools* (Board of Education 1904), which imposed a common curriculum for all schools in receipt of state support. These were in force for three years but had a massive long-term impact. Similarly, the shift towards comprehensive secondary schooling during the 1960s and 1970s was based in part on a belief in communality, which necessarily meant a shared experience of schooling and common curricula. It is clear, too, that the National Curriculum introduced by Margaret

Thatcher as part of the 1988 Education Reform Act involved some kind of reaffirmation of a common experience of schooling, despite her efforts to establish schools that were distinctive. But, in reality, at any moment since the mid-nineteenth century, any visitor to England would have been struck more by what was common to schools than by how much they differed in curriculum. Certainly, those using the schools had a distinct sense of social class, of which schools were most effective in delivering a 'good' curriculum, and this view determined local property prices and much of the nature of suburban development in Britain. That sense of competitiveness is also an enduring feature. But it is worth remembering that in order to be seen as 'successful', any school would inevitably seek to mirror best practice, not least in matters of the curriculum. In brief, it is this social competitiveness which has made lasting curriculum distinctions a complete impossibility.

Teaching method

For many years, questions of teaching method were the great unspoken assumption of English education. Certainly during the late nineteenth and early twentieth centuries there were debates on teaching method involving such leading educationalists as Quick (1898) and Adams (1936), but conducted in private. In this field, as in many others, it was widely accepted that the professionals knew best. Indeed, the 1944 Education Act did not use the word 'curriculum' but was focused entirely on the structure of the system, which was seen as the proper arena for political differences.

So why, following the reforms of the period immediately after the Second World War, involving the introduction of novel methods of teaching and the complete restructuring of secondary education, did society become increasingly unwilling to acquiesce in whatever settlement the teaching profession imposed upon it? One explanation is that society was becoming more consumerist. Individuals became accustomed to exercising choice in areas in which people had pre-viously been told what was best for them. Changes in the media facilitated the politicisation of education policy in a way that had been impossible before 1939. Education was likely to become more politicised anyway as it demanded a steadily increasing percentage of national spending. Parents, meanwhile, became anxious when they saw their children undergoing experiences that were in stark contrast to their own classroom memories. These are all necessary elements in explaining the rise of a 'new right' in education and the imposition of a new educational order under Margaret Thatcher, John Major and Tony Blair. At another level, however, many of the ingredients for increased parental concern about their children's schooling and for a sharper political interest in the details of educational practice had been in place for some time. The social functions of schooling had not changed and we know from well-established research that good schools have impacted on house prices in their immediate locality since before the end of the nineteenth century (see e.g. Marsden 1987; Goodenow and Marsden 1992).

Another element in the recent debate on teaching method is the subtle tension between the interests of parents and those of the government of the day. It is usual for governments to invoke parental power in educational reform programmes. But, in reality, what gov-ernment appears to give with one hand it often takes away with the other. Margaret Thatcher's appeal to parental involvement, for example, was underpinned by the claim that the maintenance of educational standards was a government responsibility.

To summarise, the subtle shifts in the control of classroom practices since the Second World War are intimately related to questions of teaching method. For more than 30 years after the 1944 Education Act, the teaching profession itself held sway. Politicians and parents were loath to question classroom practice, notwithstanding the unprecedented advocacy of 'child-centred' approaches, of discovery methods, the use of projects and of more informal classroom arrange-ments. Although the ORACLE project at the University of Leicester was to throw doubt on how widespread in practice were these approaches (Galton 1987), the vast majority of public pronouncements, from teacher educators and others, called for one or other version of a more progressive approach. During the 1960s and 1970s, some more extreme versions of this advocacy called for pupils themselves to become the arbiters of their own learning. Lawrence Stenhouse's Humanities Curriculum Project saw the role of the teacher as overseer rather than didact and gave pupils control of their own curriculum (Schools Council 1969). The belief that the pupil should take control in this way never became widespread, and was dealt a heavy blow by publicity surrounding Islington's William Tyndale Primary School in 1975. Here, parents objected to the teachers opting for an extreme version of child-centred education, many moving their children to neighbouring schools. The Auld Report into what had gone on (Auld 1976) seemed to link progressivism to left-wing politics and did untold harm to the cause of those advocating more liberal approaches in the classroom. In the same year, the Bennett Report (Bennett 1976) was used by the press to claim that pupils did better in primary schools that were formally organised and heavily didactic. The issue was becoming politicised.

These developments, together with the impact of the Black Papers, published between 1969 and 1977, were the cue for government to become more involved. James Callaghan's widely publicised Ruskin speech in the autumn of 1976 insisted that there was a limit to the amount the state could afford to spend on education, and, equally, that schools should be more accountable. After this came the curbing of local authority powers, the closer regulation and scrutiny of teachers, the introduction of a national curriculum that curtailed possibilities for experiment in the classroom and the strengthening of inspectorial arrangements.

The post-1945 era has seen, at different moments and in different contexts, teachers, pupils, local authorities, central government, the Inspectorate, school governors and parents being thought of as the best arbiters of classroom practice. The period after the Second World

War, in which the teachers themselves, and to a lesser extent the pupils, called the tune can be seen as a high point for child-centred approaches. Equally, the imposition of greater control by central government has meant less freedom to experiment, a greater focus on the core curriculum and basic skills, and more answerability through external checks and controls. Much of this has focused on the structure of the school day rather than on the details of classroom method and pedagogy, the introduction in 1998 of the 'literacy hour' in all primary schools being one example. There is much in this that bears an uncanny resemblance to nineteenth-century contests over schooling.

Further considerations and conclusions

The reasons why these changes took place when they did are complex, but those from the 1970s and 1980s coincided with new, and significant, approaches to educational research. Much of the reform of education during the post-war years was underpinned by research at the macro-level, social surveys which took a wide sweep and were heavily focused on issues of access and social class. Under the influence of intellectuals such as Tawney and Beveridge, researchers, not least Jackson and Marsden, Douglas, Mays, Halsey and Floud (Lowe 1988: 146) provided the intellectual ammunition for those seeking to work towards a more egalitarian provision of education. For many, this meant more open approaches in the classroom.

Elsewhere, other strategies, which were to increasingly dominate educational discourses of the 1970s and 1980s, were being devised. First, two Americans, Dan Flanders and E.J. Amidon, in what they later claimed was no more than a casual conversation in Wellington, New Zealand, in 1957, determined to establish the criteria for a closer analysis of what actually went on in the classroom. Their collaboration with J.B. Hough resulted in a voluminous 'classroom analysis' or, more precisely, 'interaction analysis' literature. Flanders explained in one book that their aim was to 'explain the variability of teacher influence'

(Flanders 1967). British researchers such as Paul Croll, Neville Bennett, Michael Bassey and Maurice Galton can all be seen as working in the shadow of this pioneering American work. Their influence on the focus of policy was to be very significant during the 1970s and 1980s.

Second, two other American researchers, Bloom and Krathwohl, were setting out at about the same time to construe their own account of the teaching process. Their focus was less on the classroom exchange and more on the identification of teacher objectives. Their most important work, *A Taxonomy of Educational Objectives* (Bloom and Krathwohl 1964), laboriously drew up a list – or taxonomy – of educational goals. It is hard to understate the significance of these initiatives for the debate on schooling in Britain. They not only played a large part in the collapse of macro-theoretical approaches to the sociology of education, but they enabled teachers and educationalists to think in terms of objectives, as never before. It was not long before these 'objectives' were reworked as 'outcomes', and a whole new slant to educational policy and planning became possible. If the aims of the teacher could now be more precisely articulated, what was more natural than the setting of 'targets' by politicians to identify how well they had been met in practice? The devices for a gradual increase in the checks and controls operating on the teaching profession were almost imperceptibly coming into place.

A number of recent initiatives have resurrected the time-honoured tradition of governments seeking to ensure diversity in school curricula. First, the city technology colleges, announced at the 1986 Conservative Party conference, were set up to provide a strong emphasis on technological, scientific and practical work which would be part-sponsored by private business. The City Technology Colleges Trust was set up in 1987 and, one year later, Kingshurst School in Solihull, West Midlands, became the first such college. In 1994, all secondary schools were invited to take on a specialist role and, thus far, over 2,000 schools have responded as the incentives have been increased and the range of acceptable specialisms widened. On taking power in 1997, Tony Blair promised continuity in this policy of encouraging specialism at secondary level and in 2003 the Trust was redesignated the Specialist Schools Trust. Meanwhile, the city academies, which had been introduced in 2000 to raise standards in the most disadvantaged areas, again with financial support from the private sector, were in 2005 rolled into this scheme through a further redesignation as the Specialist Schools and Academies Trust. Finally, in the October 2005 White Paper, *Higher Standards, Better Schools for All*, the government proposed that all schools should be run by 'a self-governing trust . . . with independence and freedom to innovate . . . to determine its own admissions policy, to determine curriculum and to choose specialisms and expansion plans'. The role of local authorities is to be changed from being 'a provider of education' to 'a more strategic commissioning role . . . a champion for the needs of parents' with 'a focus on driving up standards rather than the day to day running of individual schools' (DfES 2005: 7–12). Behind this welter of changes there is a striking parallel with what went on in the nineteenth and early twentieth centuries.

It is important to step back from this account of a whirlwind of political activity to reflect on the underlying and persistent controversies around the education system. In our context these include, over the whole period during which the State has taken an interest in schooling, issues around where power and decision-making should lie: at central or local government level or with one or other of the interested local parties? They include persistent questions about whether the focus should be on a core curriculum, on basic skills or on a wider educational experience. They include questions around how far the curriculum should be common for all pupils or to what extent, at what ages and in which directions should children specialise. They include the question of how far it is the proper job of the schools to service the immediate needs of the economy. And they include, too, the vexed question of who should take prime responsibility for determining the day-by-day curriculum and teaching methods. All these issues are as relevant and as fiercely contested now as they have been for the past two centuries.

Understanding these power struggles requires consideration of the deeper social functions of schooling. Beyond simply instructing their pupils, inculcating appropriate attitudes and skills, and working towards social cohesion (all immediately apparent functions of an education system), one other key function of schools over the last two centuries has been the inter-generational defence of social or economic advantage. Either wittingly or unwittingly, parents have used the formal education of their children as a way of ensuring that their life chances are enhanced. This means ensuring, to the best of any parent's ability, that their child goes to what is seen to be a 'good' school, 'good' being defined by its ability to provide the appropriate skills, habits or accent for whatever career and lifestyle is thought to await the child. In many cases, this has involved the relocation of parents to an address which will give access to a desirable school. This indirect price rationing of education through the housing market, which has gone on, in Britain at least, for more than a century, makes irrelevant much discussion of the rights and wrongs of private, as against state, education, since significant parts of the public provision are effectively privatised through house prices. I have addressed this issue in greater length elsewhere (Lowe 2005), but it is necessary to refer to it here to offer any meaningful explanation of the ways in which the content of the curriculum, the provision of specialist schools and the control of school curricula are contested in an industrial or post-industrial society. To offer two rhetorical questions which highlight this dilemma: What would happen if every parent in a particular city or region wanted their children all to go to the same specialist school? And what would happen if all parents had the same power to influence which schools their children attended? It is the inability to provide any meaningful answer to these paradoxes that points towards an answer to the issues addressed in this chapter.

It follows that there is no simple, or single or straightforward answer to the questions posed at the outset. For each individual, the answers lie in their own particular understandings of the social functions of formal schooling. Depending on their political persuasion or their view of society, people will take quite different views of whether or not all children should follow the same curriculum, of how far they should specialise and at what points in their education, of exactly what that curriculum should be and of who should be the major influences on what goes on in school. Similarly, the question of where power should lie in the making of these decisions has been contested from the time of the first industrial revolution and is likely to remain so. But anyone with a serious interest in schooling, whether as parent, provider or observer, should have some understanding of their own position on these issues and be able to answer the questions 'what should children be taught?', 'how should they learn?' and 'who should decide?'. And it would be easier to defend their answers if they were also able to clarify which of the social functions of schooling they see as most significant and what is their concept of the model society. An understanding of history can help us towards a better set of responses to these questions, and the history of schooling, in its social context, can help us understand why certain views of these issues seem to be in the ascendant at particular times.

References

Adams, J. (1936) *Modern Developments in Educational Practice*. London: University of London Press.

Aldrich, R. (1996) *Education for the Nation*. London: Cassell.

Amidon, E.J. and Hough, J.B. (eds) (1967) *Interaction Analysis: Theory, research and application*. Reading, MA: Addison-Wesley.

Auld, R.E. (1976) *The William Tyndale Junior and Infant Schools: Report of the public inquiry*. London: ILEA.

Bennett, N. (1976) *Teaching Styles and Pupil Progress*. London: Open Books.

Bloom, B.S. and Krathwohl, D.A. (1964) *A Taxonomy of Educational Objectives: The classification of educational goals*. London: Longman.

Board of Education (1904) *Regulations for Secondary Schools, 1904–5*. London: HMSO.

Chandos, J. (1984) *Boys Together: English public schools, 1800–1864*. London: Hutchinson.

Department for Education and Skills (DfES) (2005) *Higher Standards, Better Schools for All. More choice for parents and pupils* (White Paper, Cm 6677). London: The Stationery Office.

Flanders, N.A. (1967) 'Introduction'. In E.J. Amidon and J.B. Hough (eds) *Interaction Analysis: Theory, research and application.* Reading, MA: Addison-Wesley.

Galton, M. (1987) 'Change and continuity in the primary school: the research evidence'. *Oxford Review of Education,* 13(1), 81–93.

Goodenow, R.K. and Marsden, W. (eds) (1992) *The City and Education in Four Nations.* Cambridge: Cambridge University Press.

Johnson, R. (1970) 'Educational policy and social control in early Victorian Britain'. *Past and Present,* 49, 96–119.

Lowe, R. (1988) *Education in the Post-war Years: A social history.* London: Routledge.

— (ed.) (2000) *History of Education: Major themes* (5 volumes). London: RoutledgeFalmer.

— (2002) 'Presidential address. Do we still need history of education: is it central or peripheral?' *History of Education,* 31(6), 491–504.

— (2005) *Whatever Happened to Progressivism? The demise of child-centred education in modern Britain.* London: Institute of Education.

Maclure, J.S. (1965) *Educational Documents, England and Wales 1816–1963.* London: Methuen.

— (1984) *Educational Development and School Building: Aspects of public policy, 1945–73.* Harlow: Longman.

Marsden, W. (1987) *Unequal Educational Provision in England and Wales.* London: Woburn Press.

Ministry of Education (1947) *The New Secondary Education* (Pamphlet 9). London: HMSO.

Quick, R.H. (1898) *Essays on Educational Reformers.* London: Longmans Green.

Ringer, F. (1979) *Education and Society in Modern Europe.* Bloomington: Indiana University Press.

Rousseau, J.J. (1911) *Emile.* London: Dent (originally published in 1780).

Schools Council (1969) *Humanities for the Young School Leaver: An approach through history.* London: Evans and Methuen.

Scruton, R. (1980) *The Meaning of Conservatism.* London: Penguin.

Silver, H. (1965) *The Concept of Popular Education.* London: MacGibbon and Kee.

Simon, B. (1960) *The Two Nations and the Educational Structure, 1780–1870.* London: Lawrence and Wishart.

— (1965) *Education and the Labour Movement, 1870–1920*. London: Lawrence and Wishart.

— (1974) *The Two Nations and the Educational Structure, 1780–1870*. London: Lawrence and Wishart.

— (1991) *Education and the Social Order, 1940–1990*. London: Lawrence and Wishart.

Sylvester, D. (1970) *Educational Documents 800–1816*. London: Methuen.

8 Sowing the seeds for the National Literacy Strategy: reading debates in England, 1968–79

Roger Openshaw and Janet Soler

Introduction

As Richard Aldrich once perceptively observed, the belief that literacy standards were better in the past has considerable nostalgic appeal. He also warned that allegations of declining standards from both the left- and right-wing press pose a particular problem for curriculum historians (2000: 43). In examining the origins of a major English literacy crisis from its beginnings in the late 1960s through to the beginning of the Thatcher era, our chapter draws upon Aldrich's critical insights. This period began the trend towards the politicisation of literacy education and government intervention in what had formerly been the province of schools and local education authorities (LEAs). This, in turn, was to sow the seeds for skills-based, centralised, assessment-driven policies for the literacy curriculum. An examination of the processes surrounding the debates over literacy standards in this period, therefore, also enables a finer-grained understanding of a period that witnessed 'a rebirth of radical, non-consensual Conservatism in education' (Jones 1989: 100).

Prelude to crisis

Although concerns over literacy standards in post-war England emerged almost immediately after the conclusion of hostilities, politicians and the national press displayed only sporadic interest (Soler and Openshaw 2006: chapters 2 and 3). From the late 1960s, however, heightened concern over the social consequences of illiteracy fused with renewed attacks on progressive education, with significant implications for literacy policy. In his analysis of post-war policy, Knight highlights the activities of what he terms the 'preservationists', an increasingly influential grouping of *Conservative educationalists* (or 'CEs') that included such key figures as Rhodes Boyson, Anthony Dyson, Gilbert Longden and Brian Cox. A number of this group had been Labour Party members or supporters during the early 1960s before becoming disenchanted with progressivist educational philosophies. Instead, they promoted a vision of high culture through academic excellence and respect for subject-based knowledge (Knight 1990: 48).

The political debate over progressivism that re-emerged from the late 1960s was sharpened by the publication of the 1967 Plowden Report (DES 1967). This was 'warmly welcomed' by Labour's Secretary of State, Anthony Crosland (Simon 1991: 365), but the Opposition, influenced by preservationist arguments, signalled concerns about literacy standards when, in May 1967, a survey in London primary schools was announced by the new Conservative leadership of the Inner London Education Authority (ILEA) (*The Times*, 10 May 1967: 2). The next year saw publication of a *Daily Mirror*-sponsored book, provocatively entitled *Crisis in the Classroom* (Smart 1968). Contributors to the book included Christopher Chataway, the ILEA chairman, Boyson and Keith Gardner, a leading literacy expert. Gardner was sceptical of the tendency to use national survey figures to demonstrate that reading standards had improved in the past 20 years. He argued that colleges of education had failed to instruct entrants in how to teach reading, and consequently this area of school work lacked method and system. For some teachers, there was a strong

146

conviction that this was something to be acquired, rather than taught. The book, and the perceived complacency of the Department of Education and Science (DES), prompted concerns from both sides of the House of Commons.

Extending the literacy debate

The period 1969–76 witnessed a steep rise in concern over literacy standards and progressive education in the national press and Parliament. A major catalyst for the debate was undoubtedly the publication of the first of the so-called Black Papers, which was prefaced with an open letter to Members of Parliament (MPs), casting doubt on such approaches as 'free play', the abolition of streaming and comprehensive education (Cox and Dyson 1969: 1–6). On the inside cover of the document the editors reproduced a quote from Reginald Maudling, questioning the erosion of traditional discipline and standards, both in education and the wider society. Stephen Ball, citing Raymond Williams, argues that the basis of this type of critique reflected the tradition of 'old humanism', which 'contains both a defence of the elitist, liberal curriculum and an attack on the de-stabilising effects of progressivism' (Ball 1990: 24).

In the wake of the first Black Paper the Conservative MP Gilbert Longden was unable to obtain from Education Secretary Edward Short reliable statistics for the number of children leaving school unable to read (Hansard, HC (series 5) vol. 794, col. 175, 22 January 1970, written answer). The national press was, at this time, both reflecting and amplifying concerns over reading standards. For example, in September 1969 *The Times* revealed that 'informed critics' had sent letters claiming that, in the most recent survey conducted in 1964, about 20 per cent of all 11-year-olds read less well than the average child of 9, whilst almost half had a reading ability below that of an average 8-year-old. The education correspondent took a relatively critical view of such claims, however, which ran contrary to both the 'sober facts' of post-war reading surveys and the views of Her Majesty's Inspectorate (HMI) (*The Times*, 6 September 1969: 8). Literacy concerns, moreover, tended to focus specifically on inner-London schools, where Asian immigration was high and the proportion of poor readers was twice the national average. In November 1969, the ILEA asked the DES for a full inquiry into teacher training, following the release of a survey revealing that only one in eight junior teachers had specific training in the teaching of reading (ibid., 18 November 1969: 2). The stance taken in these articles was broadly positive about the educational achievements of the previous decade and did not, at this point, link literacy standards to preservationist, anti-progressive views, nor did they support the view that literacy standards were declining.

Renewed attacks on progressivism

The 1970s were to witness dramatic developments, both in the nature of parliamentary debates over literacy and in the reporting of reading by major newspapers such as *The Times* and *The Times Educational Supplement* (*TES*). A key reason for this radical shift in debate clearly lay in the successful lobbying by preservationists of the Conservative Party central organisation, which, in turn, gradually absorbed the philosophy into official party thinking (Knight 1990: 68).

With the Tories in power, plans proceeded for an inquiry into the teaching of reading in schools. Like the Conservatives before them, however, the Labour Opposition also sought to put school literacy shortcomings and the role of the government under a critical spotlight. In May 1971, in response to a written question from Renee Short, a Labour MP, on the levels of illiteracy among secondary school leavers, Education Secretary Margaret Thatcher observed that 'illiteracy' could not be exactly defined. She conceded that official information had been threadbare since an improvement in post-1948 literacy standards had been described in '*Progress in Reading*' – in fact, she was referring to *Standards of Reading 1948 to 1956* (Ministry of Education 1957), a pamphlet that had been frequently cited by her predecessors in response to similar questions – but advised that the results of the latest National Foundation for Educational Research (NFER) survey would be available later in the year (Hansard, HC (series 5) vol. 817, col. 217, 17 May 1971, written answer).

Labour also increased the pressure on the new government to deal more effectively with the emerging dyslexia issue. The existence of a growing public lobby on behalf of dyslexic children stimulated debate on the issue that was to intensify, with Labour arguing that dyslexia was a specific problem demanding further research, and the Conservatives claiming that the term was a catch-all for reading problems of a general nature. Nevertheless, Conservative MPs added their concerns about dyslexia, forcing William van Straubenzee, the junior Education minister, to explain that, while support for dyslexic children was normally provided within mainstream schools, some LEAs were meeting the costs of such children to attend special centres or independent schools (Hansard, HC (series 5) vol. 820, col. 173, 1 July 1971, written answer).

An indication of the extent to which attitudes towards the monitoring of literacy standards, and the government's role in maintaining them, were changing occurred in February 1972, with the release of the NFER report. This presented the results of a national survey on reading comprehension, undertaken in 1970–1 at the request of the DES (Start and Wells 1972). Whilst emphasising the uncertainty surrounding the results obtained, the report conceded that there was a high probability that the reading comprehension standard of juniors had declined somewhat since 1964, although the mean scores of both juniors and older children had undergone no significant rise or fall. The report emphasised that a multiplicity of methods, curricula and content was a striking feature of the British curriculum scene, but it could offer no explanation as to why the post-war improvement in reading standards had apparently ceased (ibid.).

The somewhat ambiguous tones of the NFER survey fuelled the political reaction that followed. An editorial in the *TES* reported an address by Thatcher to the National Union of Teachers in April 1972, in which she noted that this was the first time reading standards had not improved since regular testing began in 1938. The editorial went on to commend Thatcher for signalling her intention to appoint a committee – to be chaired, it was announced subsequently, by Sir Alan Bullock, vice-chancellor of Oxford University – to inquire into the teaching of reading in schools. Significantly, the editorial went on to link the lack of reading improvement with progressive teaching methods (*TES*, 5 April 1972, editorial: 13).

At this point, the Conservative government was still no more able than its predecessors to supply the House with any reliable estimate of the numbers of children unable to read at the age of transfer to secondary school and upon leaving full-time education: 'The Department does not collect information which would enable it to make such estimates', van Straubenzee advised (Hansard, HC (series 5) vol. 837, col. 505, 26 May 1972, written answer). The appointment, in November 1972, of the preservationist-minded Norman St John-Stevas as Parliamentary Under-Secretary of State for Education and the subsequent Conservative general election defeat of March 1974 were events that further galvanised the party into moving the education debate away from the kind of institution children attended, and towards the kind of education they actually received (Knight 1990: 73, 75). This was to further impact on the literacy standards debate because an influential body of political opinion with direct access to the media was now actively seeking to relate concerns over the teaching of reading to the wider controversy over progressive teaching methods and the alleged decline in academic standards.

The heightening of this debate can be linked to wider social events of the period. The oil price rises of the early 1970s had accentuated the UK's long-term economic decline, leading to widespread youth unemployment. A range of other incidents may also have contributed to the coming of the so-called Great Debate over education (Simon 1991: 414). For example, newly trained teachers entered a tight job market with no guarantees of finding a position, and those in posts threatened industrial action over pay and conditions, a situation only partially addressed by the 1974 Houghton Report (*TES*, 20 December 1974: 3, 5). Meanwhile, the attention of the nation centred on a small ILEA primary school, where teachers set out to operate 'what some interpret[ed] as an extreme version of the Plowden Committee's philosophy of "child-centred" education' (Simon 1991: 444–5), bringing the longstanding debate over progressivism to a head. In October 1975 the ILEA launched a full public inquiry into the 'Tyndale Affair'.

In turn, the increasingly polarised controversy over educational progressivism galvanised political interest in the Bullock Committee's work, and pressure grew for its publication. In the *TES*, coverage of the literacy standards debate from late 1974 demonstrated a tendency amongst commentators to politicise educational controversy to link literacy issues with progressivism. In December 1974 *TES* correspondent Tom Howarth, a former head of St Paul's School and a preservationist, responded to a recent tabloid article citing a primary school head's opinion that it did not matter when a child learned to read properly, as long as this was before leaving school. Howarth questioned: 'what can a parent do if he finds his child involved in a school, operated according to a theory which he might well regard as bordering on the insane?' (*TES*, 20 December 1974: 4).

Literacy skills and government intervention

Despite the controversy over progressivism, the Bullock Report, published on 18 February 1975, found 'no evidence of a large body of teachers committed to the rejection of basic skills'. It warned that improvements in the teaching of reading would come not from the acceptance of simplistic statements about methods, but rather was dependent on first defining what was meant by reading (DES 1975: 1–35). The report also noted that 'there appears to be little substance in the generalisations that large numbers of schools are promoting creativity at the expense of basic skills' (ibid.: 515; Corbett 1978: 59).

Newspapers were sharply divided regarding exactly what the Bullock Report *had* concluded about reading standards. The *Daily Mail* observed that the report found evidence indicating a decline in standards among 7- and 11-year-olds over the preceding decade, citing criticism of young teachers who had misunderstood modern 'permissive' principles to the extent that they believed that they should never directly teach children. In the same issue, Bullock Committee member Stuart Froome, an ex-junior school headmaster with 46 years' teaching experience, was quoted as saying that the final report had been dominated by progressive educators who dared not admit how low standards had actually sunk because 'that would be to say the methods employed for the past 30 years were wrong' (*Daily Mail*, 19 February 1975: 10). By contrast, the *Guardian* tended to highlight the positive conclusions of the Bullock Report, together with testimony from selected reading experts and teachers who emphasised the need to motivate beginning readers, the case for a mixture of methods to teach reading, the importance of the teacher having a love of books, and the key role played by high standards of professional practice (*Guardian*, 18 February 1975: 19). The *Guardian* hoped this 'should end the sterile debate that has been rumbling on since the start of the decade, and allow everybody to explore the means of improving literacy to which Bullock has pointed' (ibid., 19 February 1975: 12).

Some contemporary commentators identified a theme in the Bullock Report that foreshadows the gradual limitation of teacher autonomy and the external monitoring of standards from this point. The first of its 333 recommendations was for the introduction of 'a system of monitoring' both to assess a wider range of attainments than had been attempted in the past and to allow new criteria to be established for the definition of literacy (DES 1975: 513). One commentator noted that the external monitoring of standards for 11- to 17-year-olds was a particularly significant Bullock recommendation that would 'provide an ongoing estimate of literacy standards' (Corbett 1978: 59).

It is significant that, directly after the appearance of the Bullock Report, politicians on both sides of the Commons called for centralised testing and monitoring of reading standards. But Ernest Armstrong, the junior minister, could promise only that the Bullock recommendations would be 'studied carefully by the [Education] Department's assessment of performance unit' (APU) (Hansard, HC (series 5) vol. 887, cols. 177–8, 26 February 1975, written answer). In the chamber, Rhodes Boyson pressed Education Secretary Reginald Prentice about the action he proposed to take in the wake of Bullock. The answer was somewhat evasive. Prentice expressed satisfaction that the report had 'demolished many of the scare stories which had been current about the declining standards', but also admitted that education standards were not high enough (ibid., col. 1248, 4 March 1975, oral answer).

Re-emergence of the Black Papers

In early 1975 the Black Paper movement re-emerged, in conjunction with the Conservative Party's own 'Fight for Education' campaign (Knight 1990: 96–9; Simon 1991: 442) and extensive broadsheet and tabloid newspaper coverage of issues associated with reading standards (e.g. *Daily Telegraph*, 3 January 1975: 2; *Daily Mail*, 18 January 1976: 6). By the mid-1970s, the Great Debate and the accompanying media coverage were highlighting arguments against progressivism and the need to address falling literacy standards.

Black Paper 1975, like its predecessors, included contributions from a diverse mix of educationalists, writers, journalists and academics. The 'Black Paper Basics', listed in ten points on the first page, indicated that the writers were drawn together by uneasiness about progressive reforms in education, concerns for freedom of speech, high academic standards and 'open debate', and by a wish to resist illiteracy and 'social engineering' (Cox and Boyson 1975: 3). Chapters by Stuart Froome and George Weber, the latter being an officer of the Council for Basic Education, focused upon the decline of reading standards. The contributions of the editors addressed vouchers (Boyson) and examinations (Cox), and foreshadowed debates that became prominent in the following decade.

Once again, the Black Papers became a focus for parliamentary debate about literacy standards, with concern from all political sides. Boyson boasted that the recent Black Paper was the sixth best-selling paperback in the country, but Prentice was more sanguine. He welcomed educational discussion, but had not found the Black Paper 'helpful or constructive' because it took 'no account of the tremendous achievement of the majority of our teachers, who do devoted work of a very high standard, which is rising year by year' (Hansard, HC (series 5) vol. 891, cols. 1189–90, 6 May 1975, oral answer). Boyson's co-editor, Brian Cox, meanwhile, claimed that the Black Papers had 'alerted parents to declining standards in schools'. He called for teachers to return to formal reading instruction and to 'reassert their authority' (*Daily Telegraph*, 13 January 1975: 5), so prompting further articles and correspondence about these matters (e.g. ibid., 18 January 1975: 16).

Politicisation of the reading standards debate

The politicised and alarmist nature of the reading standards debate was strongly reflected in the *TES*. The front-page lead article of 31 October 1975 lamented that 'this edition of the *TES* abounds in public inquiries and tribunals, in rancorous dissension among professional colleagues and in allegations of witch-hunts on the one hand and under-bedded reds on the other'. It noted that the Tyndale inquiry had opened; that a dispute at Fircroft College had swapped allegations of paternalism with counter-allegations of radical militancy; that in Kent the LEA was dealing with a case of a teacher at odds with colleagues; whilst at South Bank Polytechnic a dispute between staff and administrators represented the latest quarrel between the Association of Teachers in Technical Institutions and the Association of Polytechnic Tutors (*TES*, 31 October 1975: 1).

The debate about educational standards was inexorably shifting towards an emphasis upon reading and reading skills, rather than simply reflecting a concern over the cultured, literate individual, as embodied in the original preservationist stance. A subsequent *TES* report of a Commons debate quoted the view of Janet Fookes, Conservative MP for Plymouth, that 'Education colleges had been too concerned with the philosophy of education and not enough with the practical craft of teaching' (ibid., 28 November 1975: 6).

There was further controversy, too, about the situation in London, where the ILEA education officer, Dr Eric Briault, contested allegations that secondary school reading standards were poor. In 1973, he contended, the average reading standard of 26,000 inner-city children in one year group rose to 98 on the 'EH2' reading comprehension test, only three points below the national average. Two years previously, the same children whilst at primary school had averaged only 94.2 (ibid., 7 November 1975: 3). This optimistic account was challenged by Robert Vigars, leader of the ILEA Conservative Opposition, and by a *TES* correspondent, G.E. Bookbinder, an educational psychologist for Salford LEA and critic of variations in reading tests (e.g. Bookbinder 1970). Bookbinder cast doubt upon the reliability of the test, the use of which signalled the ILEA's lack of confidence in the ability of its teachers to distinguish between average and poor readers (ibid., 21 November 1975: 4, 19). But Harvey Hinds, chairman of the ILEA Schools Sub-Committee, maintained that the reading standards of the children tested had unquestionably improved, and that secondary schools had reduced the proportion of poor readers from 18.4 to 13.2 per cent. Other correspondents took issue with Vigars and Bookbinder, too (*TES*, 12 December 1975: 6, 14).

The politicisation of reading standards accelerated in 1976. In April of that year James Callaghan succeeded Harold Wilson as Labour prime minister. He came under immediate pressure from his own party to pursue a decisive policy in the wake of a Lancaster University report, authored by Neville Bennett, which was given considerable media coverage. This argued that 'formal' methods of teaching were more effective than the informal type associated with the Plowden Report (Bennett 1976). In the Commons, Margaret Jackson,

155

the Under-Secretary of State for Education, confirmed that her department and the Inspectorate were closely studying Bennett's report (Hansard, HC (series 5) vol. 912, col. 1172, 8 June 1976, oral answer) and, on the same day, indicated that she was looking to schools and LEAs to respond to those Bullock recommendations that would not involve additional costs (ibid., cols. 648–9, written answer). In the following month the much anticipated Auld Report on the Tyndale affair appeared, after which teachers, schools and LEAs faced powerful calls for greater 'accountability' (Gretton and Jackson 1976). The Tyndale episode also raised issues about the structuring of children's learning and the alleged links between progressivism, militant teachers and the radical Left (Simon 1991: 445). Traditional local autonomy over the curriculum, including the teaching of reading, was called sharply into question and the stage was set for direct government intervention in these areas.

The impetus for central control was strengthened by the tone of newspaper coverage, particularly in the *Daily Mail*. One year earlier, Max Wilkinson, its education correspondent, had written a full-page article comparing educational standards in Germany with those in British comprehensive schools, claiming that 'Too late we are finding that do-as-you-please teaching methods, contempt for exams and the doctrinaire pursuit of equality can lead into dangerous blind alleys' (*Daily Mail*, 28 June 1975: 6). In a subsequent piece Wilkinson asserted that the government had hushed up a sensational report confirming that educational standards in British schools had slipped drastically since the late 1960s. The claim was backed by the secretary of the Conservative Education Committee, who alleged that the suppressed report about the 'appalling state of affairs in basic maths, English and foreign languages' drew upon evidence from parents, employers and the universities (ibid., 3 July 1975: 1). The *Daily Mail*'s coverage of the Auld Report was similarly sensationalist, attaching the blame for 'crumbling standards' and 'mediocre pupils' to the wrong turns of progressive education (ibid., 17 July 1976: 9; 19 July 1976: 6).

Clyde Chitty has described how the widespread debate in education prompted Callaghan to plan a significant speech on educational standards. In preparation for this, the so-called 'Yellow Book', a confidential DES briefing, was prepared, which addressed such issues as the teaching of the '3Rs', the possibility of stronger departmental influence over the curriculum and the place of formal assessment. Edited extracts from the Yellow Book were deliberately leaked to the *TES*, Chitty argues, to 'prepare the educational world for the shock of the Callaghan speech' which endorsed viewpoints hitherto more closely associated with the Conservatives (Chitty 1989: 81–2; *TES*, 15 October 1976: 1–2). On 22 October the *TES* carried the full text of Callaghan's speech, delivered at a foundation stone-laying ceremony at Ruskin College, Oxford. It made clear that the Labour government had taken up the debate over literacy standards. Whilst Callaghan did not lay the blame solely on schools, he referred to 'the unease felt by parents and teachers about the new informal methods of teaching which seem[ed] to produce excellent results when they [were] in well-qualified hands but [were] much more dubious in their effects when they [were] not'. The prime minister emphasised that his remarks were not meant to be 'a clarion call to Black Paper prejudices', nor a demand for a basic curriculum (although he was inclined to think that there should be one), but rather that it would be advantageous if these concerns were aired, 'shortcomings righted or fears put to rest' (*TES*, 22 October 1976: 1, 72).

Newspaper commentaries focused on the implications of the speech for raising standards, particularly in primary schools. The *Daily Mail* headed its report '3Rs must come first, says Jim' (19 October 1976: 9), while the *Daily Telegraph* quoted Callaghan's warning that 'We cannot be satisfied with maintaining existing standards let alone observe any decline' and noted the prime minister's personal view that there should be a specified 'basic curriculum' (19 October 1976: 1).

Callaghan's Secretary of State for Education and Science, Shirley Williams, promised to 'promote debate on schools, curricula and standards to which all concerned with the education service can

contribute', and confirmed that discussions with teachers' organisations, employers, industry and the Trades Union Congress would be
shortly initiated, to be followed early in 1977 by an announcement of
the government's position on curricula and standards (Hansard, HC
(series 5) vol. 918, cols. 107, 515, 26 October, 2 November 1976, written
answers).

Reviewing the key educational events of 1976 in the final leading
article for that year, the *TES* conceded that Williams had succeeded
in putting education back into the news, but also argued that she
was 'doing this in a way which divert[ed] attention from resources
and organisation (where the Government is vulnerable) to aims and
curriculum content, where everybody has a view and is dying to
express it, and where the scapegoats are more likely to be the teachers
than the Government'. This was, it was maintained, a 'populist trick
as old as democracy'. There was no reason 'why the professionals
should accept the myth that they stole the curriculum: in truth, the
teachers were left carrying the can for the public curriculum because
the politicians and the public were only too happy to turn it over to
them' (*TES*, 31 December 1976: 1).

In July 1977 the government presented its long-awaited Green
Paper on education. Entitled *Education in Schools*, this 45-page document with a joint foreword by Williams and the Secretary of State
for Wales, John Morris, assessed the present state of schools and made
recommendations for their future development. Significantly, the
document acknowledged that 'In some schools the curriculum has
been overloaded, so that the basic skills of literacy and numeracy, the
building blocks of education, have been neglected' (DES 1977a: 2).

Conclusion

The 1977 Green Paper was to prove the thin edge of a wedge, which
was to lead inexorably to the National Literacy Strategy. Shirley
Williams immediately called upon LEAs 'to review their arrangements

for curricula in schools with the object of establishing a protected part or "core" of subjects and educational principles common to all schools' (*The Times*, 22 July 1977: 4). Subsequently, Circular 14/77 (DES 1977b) asked LEAs to report on arrangements for promoting English and mathematics within the school curriculum and the APU began to systematically collect pupil performance data in these subjects. In the final months of the Callaghan administration HMI acknowledged 'the careful work . . . being done to ensure that children become literate', but also warned that

> future improvements in reading performance probably rested on the development of a more systematic approach to teaching average and more able readers to find the books they require and to use the contents page and index to decide whether to skim or to study a text thoroughly; to follow a line of argument critically; and to look out for the implications of what is written, as well as to note the explicit information the passage contains. For this to be achieved children need to be introduced to a wide range of reading material in connection with many aspects of their work.
>
> (HMI 1978: 22)

The Conservative governments of Margaret Thatcher and John Major (1979–97), and of New Labour since 1997, have seen policies for pupil literacy develop considerably, through the implementation of the National Curriculum, key stage testing, regular and robust school inspection and the National Literacy Strategy. As this chapter has shown, reading standards and literacy skills were politicised in the crucial period 1968–79, and in the continuing debates since that time party politics has remained influential in identifying policy problems and solutions.

References

Aldrich, R. (2000) 'Educational standards in historical perspective'. In H. Goldstein and A. Heath (eds) *Educational Standards*. Oxford: Oxford University Press.

Ball, S.J. (1990) *Politics and Policy Making in Education. Explorations in policy sociology*. London: Routledge.

Bennett, N. (1976) *Teaching Styles and Pupil Progress*. London: Open Books.

Bookbinder, G.E. (1970) 'Variations in reading test norms'. *Educational Research,* 12(2), 99–105.

Chitty, C. (1989) *Towards a New Education System: The victory of the New Right?* London: Falmer.

Corbett, A. (1978) *Much To Do About Education. A critical survey of the fate of the major educational reports*. London: Council for Educational Advance.

Cox, C.B. and Boyson, R. (eds) (1975) *Black Paper 1975: The fight for education*. London: Dent.

Cox, C.B. and Dyson, A. (eds) (1969) *Fight For Education: A Black Paper*. London: Critical Quarterly Society.

Department of Education and Science (DES) (1967) *Children and their Primary Schools* (Plowden Report), 2 vols. London: HMSO.

— (1975) *A Language for Life* (Bullock Report). London: HMSO.

— (1977a) *Education in Schools: A consultative document* (Green Paper; Cmnd 6869). London: HMSO.

— (1977b) *Local Education Authority Arrangements for the School Curriculum* (Circular 14/77). London: HMSO.

Gretton, J. and Jackson, M. (1976) *William Tyndale: Collapse of a school or a system?* London: Allen and Unwin.

Her Majesty's Inspectorate (HMI) (1978) *Primary Education in England*. London: HMSO.

Jones, K. (1989) *Right Turn: The Conservative revolution in education*. London: Radius.

Knight, C. (1990) *The Making of Tory Education Policy in Post-war Britain, 1950–1986*. London: Falmer Press.

Ministry of Education (1957) *Standards of Reading 1948 to 1956* (Pamphlet 32). London: HMSO.

Simon, B. (1991) *Education and the Social Order*. London: Lawrence and Wishart.

Smart, N. (ed.) (1968) *Crisis in the Classroom*. London: Hamlyn.

Soler, J. and Openshaw, R. (2006) *Literacy Crises and Reading Policy. Our children still can't read*. London: Routledge.

Start, K.B. and Wells, B.K. (1972) *The Trend of Reading Standards*. Windsor: NFER.

9 Sorting out the 'children of gold': the policy and politics of gifted education in England

Wendy Robinson

My development as a historian of education owes much to Richard Aldrich, who has been a teacher, mentor and role model to me throughout my career in the field. His intellectual integrity, commitment to the highest quality of research and publication and his ability to constantly ask searching questions of the past and present have both inspired and guided my own work. This chapter is a result of an interesting phase of my professional career when I was working very much in the present, researching educational policy, practice and research in gifted education. Being in this position inevitably prompted me to ask historical questions about the world of gifted education and in the process to begin to uncover a historical story that has not previously been told. I would like to think that my interest in asking difficult historical questions of a contested aspect of educational provision, and also thinking about where these questions might fit within the broader spectrum of historical research in education, reflects something of the powerful legacy of Richard Aldrich.

Introduction and rationale

As with many 'new' initiatives in education, research into gifted education in Britain lacks serious historical underpinning. In the late 1960s,
Cyril Burt, a pioneer in this field, lamented both the lack of interest in,
and historical record of, gifted education in England when he wrote:
'no one can properly understand the controversies of the present day
unless he knows something of their historical origins' (Burt 1975: 9).
This oversight results both from general neglect and from ongoing
tensions around notions of elitism, discrimination, meritocracy and
egalitarianism. These have been played out in the process of social
reform over the past 150 years and have shaped the way in which
histories of education have been written. Gifted education is a challenging topic that generates considerable political and ideological
discomfort. It conjures up the maligned spectre of the intelligence
quotient (IQ), intelligence testing, social inequity and even a whiff of
eugenicism. The Platonic metaphor of the 'golden child' seems out-
dated and politically anachronistic in the modern educational context.

Historians of education have not, however, totally shied away from
researching systemic provision for differential educational ability and
there is a considerable body of respected work on children with special
educational needs: those at the so-called lower end of the ability range
(e.g. Copeland 2002). Informed by the ground-breaking work on the
history of ability, measurement, mental testing and educational selection of Gillian Sutherland (1984) and Adrian Wooldridge (1994), I will
argue that historians of education have given insufficient attention
to research into the needs of gifted children. This has been a missed
opportunity, not just for filling gaps in educational knowledge, but
also in making important connections between a set of problems that
continue to dominate the field today. These include: methods and
criteria for identifying gifted children; a dearth of relevant research;
concerns about the underachievement of gifted children, particularly
those from socially disadvantaged backgrounds; disputes over how to
cater for the needs of gifted children in the mainstream system; and

ideological and political resistance to the very concept of giftedness. This chapter seeks to locate a historical overview of gifted education in England within the context of these difficulties, drawing together the past and present. It is in three main parts. First, key historical phases in the history of gifted education will be identified. Second, the 'English model' of gifted and talented education, currently being implemented, will be outlined. Third, I will examine some recurring themes which characterise the story of gifted education in England. Over 40 years ago, Burt commented on the shortage of facts determining that the 'problem' of gifted children remained 'unexpectedly complex' (quoted in Kellmer Pringle 1970: 123–4). This chapter does not set out to provide neat answers to an extraordinarily complex historical problem, but with the 'problem' of giftedness still, in many respects, unresolved, it addresses the question of how we learn from the past.

Historical mapping

Unpicking the century-long history of English research into gifted education is not an easy task. Within mainstream secondary literature, my initial investigations proved fruitless and I wondered whether such a history existed. Yet, given the well-documented history of gifted education in the United States of America (USA), shaped by the all-pervasive influence of intelligence testing in the first half of the twentieth century, this seemed improbable. Further historical delving did uncover a story, but this is not a coherent, neat or consecutive history.

The history of gifted education in England can be characterised by four, broadly chronological, phases. These overlap and have to be understood against the backdrop of more than a century of social and educational change, much of which lies beyond the scope of this chapter.

1913–50: meritocracy, psychometrics and educational psychology

The growth and influence of educational psychology, and its impact on policy-making and practice for almost half of the twentieth century, has been extensively documented, and frequently maligned because of its perceived narrowing of educational equality in the interwar and immediate post-war years. The discipline developed partly in response to national concerns about the physical and mental health of the nation, at a time when scientific methods carried increasing weight and credibility. It was also associated with the broader national efficiency and eugenics movements (Lowe 1979; Selden 1994). Within this context, the prime focus for the psychologists' gaze was to identify, measure, test and monitor the 'degenerate' and 'retarded' child, whose intelligence would register at the bottom end of a normal curve. Today, we refer to such children as having general or specific learning difficulties. Any scrutiny of the gifted child was an incidental, though probably inevitable, by-product of this primary focus.

Ideas around hereditary ability, intelligence and psychometrics, heralded by the legacy of Galton, Binet and Simon, and first implemented in practice by Burt, offer the starting points for this story of gifted education in England. Burt, the first official educational psychologist to be appointed by the London County Council (LCC) in 1913, was interested in the psychology of individual difference and the analysis and measurement of ability variations, including the 'subnormal' and the 'supernormal'. He viewed the supernormal as the nation's most-prized asset and was worried about gifted working-class children being handicapped by the cultural poverty of their homes and family life. They were, he believed, poorly served by the 'scholarship system', which had, since the 1902 Education Act, required 25 per cent of places in fee-paying secondary schools to be made available through competitive scholarship examinations. Burt believed that tests of intellectual capacity, rather than attainment, would give these children a better chance of success, because they could cut through the barriers of cultural expectation and limited educational opportunity. As early as 1915, Burt began to collect data on the abilities and performance of the top 3 per cent of candidates sitting the LCC junior scholarship examination. Information was obtained on the children's school performance, leisure interests, parental occupations and home backgrounds. He tracked this group over a long period, mirroring, on a smaller scale, the longitudinal survey of gifted students by Terman (1925–9) in the USA.

Burt's work, and that of other educational psychologists, in developing intelligence tests designed to assess children's suitability for secondary school scholarships, became hugely popular and informed the development of interwar educational policy and ideology. Local education authorities (LEAs) looked to intelligence tests to allocate secondary school scholarships and, by the early 1920s, central government policy was also supportive (Board of Education 1924).

It was during this period, when psychometrics was on the rise, that the meritocratic ideal became a dominant force for social change. In a system that had hitherto been driven by opportunity, reward and status, determined by positioning of birth within the social hierarchy, the idea of meritocracy required an education system that rewarded intelligence and ability without favour. Psychometrics demonstrated differential intellectual ability and, allied to meritocracy, questioned elitist models of education and opportunity.

To properly contextualise the history of gifted education in England, one must first understand the critical foundation of the intelligence-testing movement and psychometrics, not least because the psychological model of testing and measuring differential ability went on to dominate the gifted field for much of the remainder of the twentieth century. Indeed, it continues to vex educationists and policy-makers today. One difficulty with this psychological testing model is that a high IQ, as measured by an intelligence test, does not necessarily equate directly to 'giftedness', and potentially offers an impoverished construct omitting such other qualities as creativity or emotional intelligence. Within the historical development of psychometrics, there was much debate over general intelligence (the 'g' factor) and specific intelligence. Whilst recognising these difficulties, Burt brought the idea of gifted children into the arena of psychological research. Limited as his research was, within an emergent system of mass secondary education, he drew attention to a 'supernormal' group of children, though their special needs and provision were not addressed. Burt's work has been criticised for its design and interpretation, but in recognising the gifted child, Burt was a significant figure.

1940s–1960s: pathologising the gifted child

In this second historical phase, which ran alongside and beyond the first, the field remained marginal and still predominantly located within an educational and child psychology-based framework. From the 1940s to the late 1960s, much published research on the gifted child focused on the measurable characteristics of individuals, tending to present them as potential victims or threats. As victims, gifted children were at risk of psychiatric and behavioural problems because of their prodigy. As threats, both to themselves and to society, the misguided gifted child was at risk of underachievement and, hence, delinquency. This reflected wider social concerns about youth delinquency and the provision of child guidance clinics, as recommended in the Underwood Report on Maladjusted Children (Ministry of Education 1955). The gifted child is pathologised through a psycho-medical model, paralleling the way in which the 'retarded' child was subject to a medical, not educational, context. More importantly, the supernormality of the gifted child, rather like the subnormality of the retarded child, highlighted its specialness or difference as something rather exotic, but also problematic.

Academic papers from this period illustrate this construction of the gifted child. One head of a private child psychiatric clinic wrote about 'Brilliant children, with special reference to their particular difficulties'

(Nevill 1937: 247), while the director of Child Guidance for Birmingham addressed the theme of 'Maladjusted children of high intelligence' (Burns 1949: 137). Other articles analysed giftedness and delinquency, particularly in boys (e.g. Simmons 1956), the effect of counselling on the achievement of high-ability pupils (Shouksmith and Taylor 1964), and the special characteristics of bright delinquents (Gath *et al.* 1970), while Kellmer Pringle published her extensive study of 'able misfits' (1970). Focusing on the psychological problems of giftedness recognised that such children were at risk of not reaching their true potential. Most studies viewed the gifted child in isolation from their educational contexts, though some perpetuated the psychological ideas of abnormality or difference.

Millfield School, in Street, Somerset, which opened as an exclusive public school in 1935, led by a pioneering headmaster, R.J.O. Meyer, developed a reputation for work with intellectually gifted pupils with behavioural problems. By the early 1960s, some LEAs were prepared to pay fees to send students in this category to Millfield. Similarly, Redhill School, in Kent, famous for its progressive approaches to education, under the leadership of Otto Shaw, became a charitable trust, recognised by the Ministry of Education for its expertise in working with 'maladjusted boys of very superior intelligence'. Like Millfield, Redhill was a boys-only establishment and worked on the principle of residential care. Kneesworth Hall School in Cambridgeshire, meanwhile, opened in the late 1940s, and developed a reputation for turning around the lives of 'intelligent delinquents'. Each of these schools was independent, but maintained a quasi-relationship with the mainstream state sector by offering a 'cure' for the 'problems' of giftedness.

1960s–mid-1990s: local, regional and voluntary activity

By the early 1960s, there was a noticeable shift in direction, with gifted education moving closer to mainstream concerns. The 1961 *Year Book of Education* reflected this interest by focusing upon 'Concepts of excellence in education' and publishing several international area studies on the education of gifted children. Mary Waddington, from the University of London Institute of Education, contributed the British overview to the volume, discussing such issues as integration, segregation, streaming, setting, curriculum differentiation and enrichment and acceleration (Waddington 1961).

The increased interest in the field was not reflected in national policymaking. In 1966, the founder members of the National Association for Gifted Children (NAGC), which has, ever since, provided voluntary support for gifted children and their parents, described experiments, based in Brentwood and Liverpool, in the hope of interesting teachers and parents (Branch and Cash 1966). The Plowden Report's brief chapter on the education of gifted children (DES 1967: 305–8) also alluded to these studies which, while differing in their approaches, both had, as a main objective, the identification of strategies which could be adapted by teachers in mainstream state primary schools.

The 'Brentwood experiment', launched in 1964, was the brainchild of Dr Sydney Bridges of Brentwood Teacher Training College. Recognising a weakness in his students' ability and confidence to meet the needs of more able pupils during school placements, a group of children, aged between 8 and 10, from four local schools, with exceptionally high IQs, attended the college for one afternoon a week. Here, selected trainees under supervision taught them in small groups. A one-year pilot preceded a refined scheme in which younger children were identified and studied over a longer period, prior to secondary school entry. The experiment worked on an enrichment model of enhanced curriculum provision and the development of higher-order thinking skills and logic. Children received an experimental type of instruction, suited, as far as possible, to the individual talents of each. It focused on attitudes towards gifted children, underachievement, underperformance, low expectations, creative and open-ended work, learning environments, peer cooperation and social and emotional needs (Bridges 1969).

The 'Liverpool experiment', described as a 'pioneer of its kind', was conducted by Professor Norton Tempest from 1967–71. Fifteen 'clever' children from a seaside town in north-west England were identified during their last year of infant school, and formed into a small class in a 'normal' primary school where, with the same teacher, they experienced an 'experimental' education, in terms of curriculum and teaching styles, until they transferred to secondary school. The monitoring of these children, over a four-year period, sought to 'furnish suggestions for the enrichment of the curriculum and examples of methods of work and general attitudes which would be helpful to teachers who have to deal with the one or two children in an ordinary primary class' (Tempest 1974: 2).

There were other, less well-documented examples of local programmes, too: Eric Laycock, of the West Sussex School Psychological Service, authored a pamphlet for local teachers in the late 1950s (Hoyle and Wilks 1974: 9), heralding the introduction of enrichment classes, which were also introduced by Essex LEA (Branch and Cash 1966: 88). In Somerset, a Brentwood-style programme was trialled at Bristol University in 1973, while in Southend, an innovative junior head teacher allocated a room for gifted children to work independently, supported by a half-time teacher (ibid.: 90).

These innovations in mainstream schools were dependent on voluntary and local initiatives. During the mid- to late 1970s, however, central government interest began to increase, coinciding with the backlash against comprehensive schools, which had largely replaced selective secondary education, and increasing concerns about educational standards. In 1974, Eric Hoyle and John Wilks, from Bristol University, published a report, *Gifted Children and their Education*, for the Department of Education and Science (DES) (Hoyle and Wilks 1974). This highlighted some political difficulties of defining and identifying giftedness – a concept that, for some, was besmirched with elitism – and painted a bleak picture of provision for gifted children in mainstream schools. A subsequent publication, *Gifted Children in Middle and Comprehensive Secondary Schools*, was the result of an examination by school inspectors of 130 schools and a range of LEA policies. It reported that giftedness was neither implicit nor explicit in the day-to-day dialogue of most schools (DES 1977: 13). It did, however, praise some pockets of regional activity and recommended that gifted children could be catered for in mainstream schools with good teachers, adequate resources, clear policies and access to specialist external agencies.

More recently, Joan Freeman (1995), a leading expert and adviser on gifted education since the mid-1970s, has argued that the assisted places scheme, introduced by the Conservative government in 1981, was an indirect policy that favoured gifted children, building on the earlier experiments with Millfield, Redhill and Kneesworth Hall. The scheme, which ran until 1997, awarded over 75,000 government scholarships, permitting the most able state primary school children to attend an independent school. But the scheme proved politically unpopular, raising concerns about social equity and equality of opportunity. Others felt that it implied that state education was second rate.

1990–present: towards the English model

The final phase, which brings the story to the present day, saw a move from organic, local initiatives to central policy-making. Straddling this shift was the Schools Council Gifted Project (1979–83), which brought together LEA initiatives and experiments, focusing on curriculum development and classroom practice, rather than identification and selection. In spite of a range of voluntary activity, largely coordinated by the National Association for Gifted Education (NAGE), established in 1984, and other voluntary associations organised by parents or for commercial purposes – such as the National Association for Able Children in Education (NACE), GIFT and Mensa – Freeman reported in 1998 that there was 'no specific overall educational policy for the gifted in Britain' (Freeman 1998: 67).

Until the development of a national strategy, and in spite of the best efforts of voluntary groups, the English education system's response to the educational needs of gifted pupils has been characterised by a long trend of low expectations at the classroom and school levels (DES 1978, 1992; Ofsted 2003). This trend was reinforced by unenthusiastic attitudes in the teaching profession and within LEAs, either on the grounds that they lacked confidence about how to challenge such students through their teaching (HMI 1992: para 3) or that meeting their educational needs had lower priority than managing the behaviour and learning of other pupils in busy and challenging classrooms, or both (House of Commons Education and Employment Committee 1999: paras 43, 50).

Ideology has played a part, also, in that making special provision for gifted and talented pupils is commonly constructed in academic discourse as elitist, reinforcing the advantages that already advantaged professional classes might gain in the competition for admission to high-status universities (Power *et al.* 2003). To these problems were added a complex set of social pressures. Parental anxiety about mainstream school provision led to high demand from the professional classes for private and, where available, selective secondary schooling (Fox 1984; Adonis and Pollard 1998), even when the advantages, in terms of educational attainment, were dubious or small (Crook *et al.* 1999). When the State provided financial support for differentiated provision, for example, via the assisted places scheme, it was clearly disproportionately accessed by those with high levels of social and intellectual capital, mainly the professional classes and those in genteel poverty (Edwards *et al.* 1989).

From this context of policy drift and socially skewed parental ambition, galvanised by the New Labour government's agenda for social inclusion, central policy began to emerge. Quasi-official interest had been reflected in a survey of provision by Her Majesty's Inspectorate (HMI), and a review of research for the Office for Standards in Education (Ofsted) (HMI 1992; Freeman 1998). More officially, in direct policy terms, the government's initiative to improve the quality of education in urban areas, *Excellence in Cities* (EiC), introduced in 1999, included specific targeting of gifted and talented pupils. Moreover, in 2001, the Department for Education and Skills (DfES) committed itself to supporting gifted and talented students in all its strategies (DfES 2001). This policy change had been framed in a House of Commons Education and Employment Select Committee report (1999), which examined issues associated with 'highly able children'. Among its recommendations were the following:

- Funding to support the education of gifted children should be incorporated into the generic funding of schools;

- All national initiatives should incorporate a gifted and talented component, clearly specified;

- Ofsted should include data on provision for gifted and talented pupils in its inspection of schools and of LEAs;

- Initial teacher training should be required to give higher priority to the education of gifted and talented pupils; and

- All schools should be required to appoint a named person as the school's coordinator for gifted and talented education.

Enrichment and extension of the normal curriculum, partnerships between schools and other agencies – such as universities, out-of-school provision, and improved use of information and communications technology – were additionally identified as benefits. The establishment of a National Academy for Gifted and Talented Youth (NAGTY) at Warwick University, in 2002, provided the organisational mechanism for leading, delivering and supporting the delivery of the policy.

At national and, indeed, international levels, the English model is presenting itself very much as a new and radical approach, committed to equity, with an ambition to counter those social and economic factors shown to have had a restrictive influence on educational achievement. It is to be hoped that this model will contribute to widening access to higher education, as well as social and economic reform in its broader sense. Deborah Eyre, the NAGTY director, has highlighted the socially inclusive imperative of the policy in the following terms:

> Traditionally gifted education has been seen as divorced from the general education system, yet if a country's education system seeks to provide appropriate education for all its children, then the education of the most able (gifted) should be seen as just one part of a larger whole. This in itself should provide a compelling case for a nationally coherent and integrated approach to the education of the gifted. However there are reasons that transcend education policy that suggest that a country would be well-advised to give gifted education a more central location. Today's gifted pupils are tomorrow's social intellectual economic and cultural leaders and their development cannot be left to chance. Where it is left to chance, evidence indicates that educational progress is not so much a question of intellectual merit but rather a question of affluence, with the most affluent receiving the best education and therefore achieving most highly.
>
> (Eyre 2004)

The recent White Paper, *Higher Standards, Better Schools for All* (DfES 2005), makes further policy commitments for gifted and talented students in respect of personalised learning, extended schooling and support for those from socially disadvantaged and ethnic minority backgrounds.

The long-term impact or success of this model is unknown. There remain ongoing questions about the appropriate identification of gifted children, how they should be properly integrated into the school, and how curricula should be developed to provide a suitably challenging intellectual diet. Efforts to meet the needs of the gifted may require schools to rethink their practices in relation to pupil grouping, differentiation, curriculum compacting and acceleration. Policies are in the process of being worked out, both on the ground by teachers and by the DfES.

Recurring themes

The chequered history of gifted education in England from the late nineteenth century illuminates some recurring themes or problematics, which time itself has not managed to resolve. These include definitions and identification, concerns about underachievement – particularly of disadvantaged young people – and political and ideological resistance to special educational provision for gifted students. In terms of understanding the field, it is important to track these issues along a historical continuum, though this will not necessarily offer neat answers or solutions.

Currently, in spite of the DfES having established criteria for the definitions and identification of giftedness and talent in school-age children, there remain problems and confusions. The EiC initiative, which targeted the improvement of school provision for gifted and talented students, required schools to identify the top 5 to 10 per cent of their cohort in terms of high attainment or latent high ability in one or more academic subjects. The thorny subject of 'talent', referring to creative, expressive or sporting prowess, is an even more contentious concept. Is giftedness generic or specific? What percentage of the population should be identified as gifted? Should it be 10, 5, 2 or 1? Jesson (2005) called for the top 5 per cent of pupils to be classified as gifted on the basis of Key Stage Two attainment tests, challenging the NAGTY view that giftedness is expertise in development and that multiple forms of data should be used in the identification process. The fundamental problem for educators, according to Strand, is the multitude of views about what constitutes giftedness or high ability, some 'experts' emphasising psychological constructs such as intelligence and creativity, but many more focusing on children who attain 'high marks in school subjects' (Strand 2006: 2).

The contested nature of identifying giftedness has been an enduring historical theme. Burt identified gifted students as those with an IQ above 130, around 2.5 per cent of the whole population, while in the USA Terman's IQ threshold was 140. Hitchfield's (1973) research, using the National Child Development Study longitudinal data for gifted children born in the first week of March 1958, preferred a mixed model of identification, using tests as well as consultation with parents, teachers and the children themselves.

Broader social issues also came into play, including the under-identification of socially disadvantaged and ethnic minority groups and the need to recognise the concept of underachievement relative to potential. A major thrust of the 'English model' is to identify and support students from groups which, historically, have encountered barriers to educational access and attainment, notwithstanding the trend towards equality of opportunity and equity in the past 50 years.

Burt, whose early research was undertaken in the context of an emerging state education system riven by inequality, was particularly concerned about able children from culturally, as well as economically, poor homes being disadvantaged by the scholarship route. He believed that tests of intelligence, rather than of attainment, were the fairest way of identifying gifted children and could neutralise the effects of bad teaching and unfavourable surroundings. Burt kept dossiers on those children who gained – or just failed to gain – scholarships and he found a wide disparity between the numbers of pupils awarded scholarships in poorer London boroughs, such as Bermondsey and Bethnal Green, compared with the relatively more affluent areas of Hampstead, Lewisham and Wentworth.

The selective system of secondary education which followed the 1944 Education Act continued to favour middle-class children, and the drive for comprehensivisation and egalitarianism, from the 1960s, failed to eradicate educational underachievement. Hitchfield's cohort of gifted children born in 1958 was found to contain a dis-proportionate number of middle-class pupils, reinforcing anxieties about unutilised and underdeveloped high ability (Hitchfield 1973: 16). Tempest, too, recognised that socially deprived children with unfavourable home circumstances were less likely to be recognised as clever. Similarly, in 1974 it was found that

At school the proportion of gifted pupils who remain unrecognised is unknown, but the evidence indicates that it is probably considerable, particularly among children coming from poor families, those living in educational priority areas, and immigrants – environmental deprivation has its most adverse effects on the scholastic performance of the brightest children, not the average or dull.

(Hoyle and Wilks 1974: 5)

Given the longstanding, and still existent, problem of educational disadvantage, it is ironic that another recurrent historical theme is ideological resistance to giftedness, long associated with elitism by professionals and academics. An 'ideological block' is still to be found in many schools, militating against the implementation of DfES and NAGTY frameworks intended to allow more able children to excel (*The Times*, 13 February 2006: 13), but confirming the endurance of the view that the ablest students are capable of managing by themselves. In 1967, Plowden identified an egalitarian suspicion of 'giftedness' (DES 1967: 305–8), Burt's foreword to *Able Misfits* acknowledged hostility towards the concepts of high and innate abilities, while Hitchfield attributed the discomfort of teachers to ancient associations between genius, the supernatural and madness (Hitchfield 1973: 106). Both Tempest and Bridges reported negative teacher attitudes and sought to promote research and training to help teachers recognise, identify and appropriately challenge gifted children as early as possible in their school careers. In 1977, a DES report similarly noted teacher indifference, a prevailing view that gifted children can look after themselves, and a reluctance among LEAs to develop policies 'which might be constructed by the local electorate as an injudicious selection of an elite' (DES 1977: 9).

In terms of the relationship between current policy and the development of the English model, the priority of which is to ensure that gifted children are properly catered for within mainstream education, there are some interesting parallels with earlier studies. Most of the twentieth-century studies were focused on identification, rather than provision. Neither Bridges nor Tempest advocated creating special schools for gifted children, nor did they visualise placing them in the independent sector. They hoped, instead, to create within the main-stream state system opportunities for the ablest children to develop. In the 1970s, it was argued that 'gifted children, on whatever criteria they are selected, stand or fall by the quality of education they receive' (Hitchfield 1973: 207), while the DES preferred gifted children to attend mainstream, rather than 'super'-selective, schools. These early ambitions are clearly reflected in the ambition and scope of the English model currently in place.

Conclusion

Notions of 'reinvented wheels', 'swinging pendulums' and the need for each generation to rework the problems of the last are frequently cited in historical analyses of education policy. But the relationship between the present and the past is rarely straightforward, linear or progressive. Clear historical perspectives and an understanding of change and continuity over time are enriching, but not in themselves sufficient to resolve the ongoing issues requiring educational reform. Perhaps this is because education is so inextricably connected with the critical nexus of economy, society, politics and ideology, each of which are themselves products of history.

Gifted education continually exposes tensions in relation to beliefs and concepts about opportunity and social inclusion. These issues have been regularly revisited and addressed as contexts influencing education have changed. During the twentieth century it is clear that this dimension of educational provision moved from peripheral, organic innovation towards centralised systemic reform. Within the frameworks of this central policy, it remains to be seen how current initiatives will impact upon the future reforms.

References

Adonis, A. and Pollard, S. (1998) *A Class Act: The myth of Britain's classless society.* London: Penguin.

Board of Education (1924) *Report of the Consultative Committee on Psychological Tests of Educable Capacity and their Possible use in the Public System of Education.* London: HMSO.

Branch, M. and Cash, A. (1966) *Gifted Children.* London: Souvenir Press.

Bridges, S.A. (ed.) (1969) *Gifted Children and the Brentwood Experiment.* London: Sir Isaac Pitman and Sons.

Burns, C.L.C. (1949) 'Maladjusted children of high intelligence'. *British Journal of Educational Psychology,* 19, 137–99.

Burt, C. (1975) *The Gifted Child.* London: Hodder and Stoughton.

Copeland, I. (2002) *The Backward Pupil over a Cycle of a Century.* London: Upfront Publishing.

Crook, S., Power, S. and Whitty, G. (1999) *The Grammar School Question: A Review of Research on Comprehensive and Selective Education.* London: Institute of Education.

Department for Education and Skills (DfES) (2001) *Schools: Achieving Success. Consultation on Education White Paper.* London: HMSO.

— (2005) *Higher Standards, Better Schools for All. More choice for parents and pupils* (White Paper, Cm 6677). London: The Stationery Office.

Department of Education and Science (DES) (1967) *Children and Their Primary Schools* (Plowden Report; vol. 1). London: HMSO.

— (1977) *Gifted Children in Middle and Comprehensive Secondary Schools.* London: HMSO.

— (1978) *Primary Education in England: A survey.* London: HMSO.

— (1992) *The Education of Very Able Children in Maintained Schools: A review by HMI.* London: HMSO.

Edwards, T., Fitz, J. and Whitty, G. (1989) *The State and Private Education: An evaluation of the assisted places scheme.* Basingstoke: Falmer Press.

Eyre, D. (2004) *Gifted Education: The English model.* University of Warwick: National Academy for Gifted and Talented Youth. Online. Available HTTP: <http://www.nagty.ac.uk/about/english_model_full.aspx> (accessed 2007).

Fox, I. (1984) 'The demand for public school education: a crisis of confidence in comprehensive schooling'. In G. Walford (ed.) *British Public Schools: Policy and practice.* Lewes: Falmer Press.

Freeman, J. (1995) *Actualising Talent.* London: Cassell.

— (1998) *Educating the Very Able: Current international research*. Ofsted Reviews of Research. London: The Stationery Office.

Gath, D., Tennent, G. and Pidduck, R. (1970) 'Educational characteristics of bright delinquents'. *British Journal of Educational Psychology*, 40, 216–19.

Her Majesty's Inspectorate (HMI) (1992) *The Education of Very Able Children in Maintained Schools: A review by HM Inspectorate*. London: HMSO.

Hitchfield, E.M. (1973) *A Long-term National Study of Able Children and their Families*. London: Longman.

House of Commons Education and Employment Committee (1999) *Highly Able Children: Third report*. London: The Stationery Office.

Hoyle, E. and Wilks, J. (1974) *Gifted Children and their Education*. London: HMSO.

Jesson, D. (2005) 'Identifying gifted and talented pupils – issues for all schools'. Paper presented to the Special Schools and Academies Trust annual conference, November.

Kellmer Pringle, M.L. (1970) *Able Misfits*. London: Longman.

Lowe, R. (1979) 'Eugenicists, doctors and the quest for national efficiency: an educational crusade, 1900–1939'. *History of Education*, 8(4), 293–306.

Ministry of Education (1955) *Report of the Committee on Maladjusted Children* (Underwood Report). London: HMSO.

Nevill, M.E. (1937) 'Brilliant children, with special reference to their particular difficulties'. *British Journal of Educational Psychology*, 7, 247–301.

Office for Standards in Education (Ofsted) (2003) *Standards and Quality 2002/03: The annual report of Her Majesty's Chief Inspector of Schools*. London: The Stationery Office.

Power, S., Whitty, G., Edwards, T. and Wigfall, V. (2003) *Education and the Middle Class*. Buckingham: Open University Press.

Selden, S. (1994) 'Early twentieth-century biological determinism and the classification of exceptional students'. *Evaluation and Research in Education*, 8(1–2), 21–39.

Shouksmith, G. and Taylor, J.W. (1964) 'The effect of counselling on the achievement of high ability pupils', *British Journal of Educational Psychology*, 34, 51–7.

Simmons, M.M. (1956) 'Intelligent delinquents'. *The Times Educational Supplement*, 2 March.

Strand, S. (2006) *Identifying Gifted Students: An evaluation of the National Academy for Gifted and Talented Youth (NAGTY) procedure*. University of Warwick: National Academy for Gifted and Talented Youth.

Sutherland, G. (1984) *Ability, Merit and Measurement: Mental testing and English education, 1880–1940*. Oxford: Clarendon Press.

Tempest, N.R. (1974) *Teaching Clever Children, 7–11*. London: Routledge and Kegan Paul.

Terman, L. (1925–9) *Genetic Studies of Genius,* Vols. I–V. Stanford: Stanford University Press.

Waddington, M. (1961) 'Problems of educating gifted young children with special reference to Britain'. In G.Z. Bereday and J.A. Lauwerys (eds) *The Year Book of Education 1961: Concepts of excellence in education*. London: Evans Brothers.

Wooldridge, A. (1994) *Measuring the Mind: Education and psychology in England, c.1860–c.1990*. Cambridge: Cambridge University Press.

10 Securing our future? National security and the history of education

Gary McCulloch

Introduction

As Richard Aldrich has insisted, there are lessons to be drawn from history, albeit that different lessons may be drawn from consideration of the same events (Aldrich 2006: 1). Aldrich himself argues persuasively that 'many of the lessons to be drawn from historical perspectives upon education must be couched in terms of caution, of thorough research and planning, of emphasising the need above all to retain that which is good while seeking to improve that which is of less worth' (Aldrich 1997: 11). It is helpful to interrogate the present through a range of historical perspectives and methods, and also to shed light on our history from our vantage point in the ever-changing present. The examples that Aldrich puts forward to demonstrate this point relate especially to such matters as school buildings, curriculum and pedagogy. We should also be enabled thereby to engage with the major and fundamental issues that have confronted past societies as well as our own (Lowe 2005). Historians of education have often been especially conscious of the need to address both past and present, although they have in many cases neglected ideas that have been developed across the humanities and the social sciences (McCulloch and Richardson 2000). It is necessary to pay due attention to all these issues in order to be able to contribute to broader debates.

It is apt to acknowledge that education often has both domestic and international implications, and not only separately, but as two sides of the same coin. Much research on education dwells on its characteristics as an aspect of domestic social policy, while there is a smaller body of work that highlights its significance as part of foreign and overseas policy, especially in the export of ideas and practices to other countries. Yet there is also another dimension that has attracted much less attention, which is the relationship between the country's changing place in the world and the nature of education and society at home. As Raphael Samuel pointed out in his discussion of the connections between the 'imperial' and the 'domestic', for example, 'Some of the more utopian strains in English life, as represented, say, in the open-air movement of the late nineteenth century, and the rise of the Boy Scouts and the Girl Guides, might also be shown to have their original location in colonising fantasies' (Samuel 1999: 95).

In the spirit of these broad aspirations, this chapter investigates the theme of 'security', and more specifically national security, which has become such a prominent aspect of society, politics and individual lives in Britain especially since the London bombings of July 2005. It examines what historians of education can contribute to this issue from their experience and expertise. In particular, it asks, first, how can we characterise the history of education in relation to the theme of security? And, second, it raises questions about what leverage we can bring to bear to help us understand our present policies and predicaments.

A key starting point for consideration in relation to this theme is the debate over security that has developed in Britain since the terrorist attacks in London on 7 July 2005. This debate has included some significant educational issues. One was the personal involvement in teaching by some of the London bombers, such as Mohammed Sidique Khan, who worked as a learning mentor for children of immigrant families at a school in Leeds (*The Times*, 14 July 2005: 1). Another was about the nature of British identity, and the ways in which schools might attempt to inculcate this further (ibid.: 8). Particular concerns were raised about higher education and its potential role in fostering extremism. Increasing amounts of money were invested in high-tech campus protection, while widespread anxieties were voiced about the possible effects of a new Terrorism Bill that was introduced at this time (*The Times Higher Education Supplement*, 16 September 2005: 2; Glees 2005). A strong sense of insecurity underlay this debate, involving calls to reinforce protection not only against physical threats from outside, but also against ideological challenges, and issues about how best to counter these.

Security in the history of education

The nature of the threat may have been unprecedented, but it was far from the first time that security issues had been raised in connection with education. In other countries, security issues have been highly familiar in educational debate. This is especially notable in the United States, where national security has been a key factor in historical development, and is being increasingly recognised for its significance in the history of education. In general terms, Richard Hofstadter's remarkable essay *The Paranoid Style in American Politics* evokes 'the qualities of heated exaggeration, suspiciousness, and conspiratorial fantasy' (Hofstadter 1966: 3) that have played such a major part in American history. According to Hofstadter, although American political life has 'rarely been touched by the most acute varieties of class conflict' it had 'served again and again as an arena for uncommonly angry minds' (ibid.: 3). Hofstadter was thinking especially of a right-wing mentality that was encouraged by the Cold War of the 1950s and articulated most strongly by Senator Joe McCarthy, but which he argued had deeper historical roots and also continuing contemporary manifestations. He suggested, for example, that 'the paranoid disposition is mobilised into action chiefly by social conflicts that involve ultimate schemes of values and that bring fundamental fears and hatreds, rather than negotiable interests, into political action. Catastrophe or the fear of catastrophe is most likely to elicit the syndrome of paranoid rhetoric' (ibid.: 39). The educational manifestations of such 'paranoia' have been emphasised especially in relation to the universities. For instance, the prominent critic Noam Chomsky and a number of colleagues have vividly recounted the effects of the McCarthy investigations on university life, the changes in government funding of scholarly work during the Cold War, and the ways in which these developments 'reshaped university structures and the content of academic disciplines' (Chomsky *et al.* 1997: xii).

Recent historical writings on education in the United States have begun to document these issues in detail. Stuart Foster's work on the 'red scare' of the 1950s has helped to lead the way forward in this area (Foster 2000). Parallels between the Cold War debates and those of today have also been emphasised in the sense that each of these debates has been influenced strongly by conservative forces in society. This direct linkage between the historical and the contemporary highlights the role of the critics of public schooling in the 1940s and 1950s, the propaganda against 'subversive' teachers and communist sympathisers in the schools and universities and the media more broadly, and the impact of such attacks on the character of education (see also, e.g. Foster and Davis 2004). John Rudolph's book *Scientists in the Classroom* (2002) is a further significant contribution to this vein of historical writing, exploring, for example, the ways in which the National Science Foundation (NSF), as the government agency responsible for ensuring the nation's scientific strength, 'found itself pressured from the top by influential members of Congress and various government committees to address programmatically the pressing issue of ensuring an adequate supply of scientific talent to meet the mounting Soviet threat' (ibid.: 58). The NSF eventually responded to this pressure and moved decisively to reform high school science education. Rudolph argues that science became integrated into the national security infrastructure of the United States, leading directly to a renewed interest in the schools.

To what extent does this theme have resonance in relation to the history of education in Britain? It is reflected in the discussions of a number of commentators at different stages during the twentieth century. One of the most interesting of these is that of Fred Clarke, a leading sociologist of education, in his book *Education and Social Change: An English interpretation*, written at the start of the Second World War (Clarke 1940). Clarke argued that the basic values and structures of education in England (he only claimed to talk about England) were rooted in a sense of national security that came from 'the days of an unchallenged British Navy, a world-wide stable economic system, an Empire whose destinies are more or less directed from London, pre-aviation insularity for Great Britain, and no wireless anywhere' (ibid.: 2). This, he suggested, had led to a 'lack of critical self-awareness'. If there was 'a master-key for the interpretation of English educational phenomena', he proposed, 'it is given in the word *Security*' (ibid.: 10). By this he meant 'the physical security, only recently impaired, of the island position', and 'the economic security guaranteed by a world-wide Empire, world-wide capital investment and the other familiar features of the nineteenth century economy' (ibid.: 10). In turn, he continued, this encouraged a habit of thinking in terms of concrete precedent rather than abstract principle, the maintenance of a well-defined social hierarchy, and the preference for a limited degree of liberty over an abstract equality. All such aspects, Clarke ventured, were rooted fundamentally in the conditions produced by 'long centuries of internal peace and external security' (ibid.: 11). And it was the threatened change to these historical conditions with the onset of the Second World War that Clarke saw as an opportunity to start rethinking and reflecting as a precursor to reform.

Many historians would concur with Clarke's view that Britain's educational history has been fundamentally shaped by the relative physical security of the country's borders, and the lack of foreign invasions over the last two centuries, leading to a general insularity, complacency and conservatism in relation to educational reform. The influential interpretation offered by Martin Wiener, for example, explained the prevailing lack of interest in vocational and technical education as being based in what he described as 'a cultural *cordon sanitaire* encircling the forces of economic development – technology, industry, commerce' (Wiener 1981: ix). This constituted a 'mental quarantine' that took shape with the social changes of the Victorian era. According to Wiener, this was reflected vividly in the dominance of the Victorian public schools, detached from the modern world of technology and business. Also, the ancient universities of Oxford and Cambridge continued to provide role models for national character that emphasised continuity and tradition (see also Hobsbawm and Ranger 1983). Thus, Wiener concluded, 'revivified public schools and ancient universities furnished the re-formed and cohesive English elite with a way of life and an outlook that gave little attention or status to industrial pursuits' (ibid.: 24). This was also the view of the military historian Correlli Barnett (1986, 1995). Barnett gave particular emphasis to the theme of national security and argued that complacency and a sense of physical and ideological security had encouraged old-fashioned and utopian thinking, dreams and illusions and a flinching from reality, rather than realistic and pragmatic responses to a rapidly shifting context.

On the surface, the key educational figure Cyril Norwood is a major example of this kind of thinking. In his book *The English Tradition of Education* (Norwood 1929) he expounded on the theme of 'knowledge and security'. According to Norwood, the control and security that would characterise the democracy of the future would be based on knowledge and its application, and the development of education would therefore be a fundamental dimension of this. It was elitist and hierarchical in nature, taking its cue from the Greek philosopher Plato. Thus, he argued, security in the future would mean 'handing over life to the guidance of those who know, not to those who are amateurs at improvisation, however brilliant, or to those who with stoical perseverance under hard knocks are content to muddle through' (ibid.: 249). At the same time, he developed a notion of national character based on the virtues found especially in the leading public schools.

His view of English educational history was one of a unique English tradition realised most fully in the public schools, and inspired in the modern era by Thomas Arnold of Rugby. This shaped an ideal of secondary education that was reflected in his major report on the curriculum and examinations in secondary schools, published in 1943 (Board of Education 1943; McCulloch 2006, 2007).

Fred Clarke, who was very suspicious of Norwood's ideas, put the idea of security under further scrutiny in his discussions with colleagues in the group 'The Moot' during the Second World War. In these discussions, the sociologist Karl Mannheim proposed the idea of 'education for change' as opposed to 'education for security', emerging as 'a new problem to be faced in the English education system' (Mannheim to Clarke, 4 November 1939, Clarke Papers, file 47, Institute of Education, University of London). It would be tempting to argue that for the remainder of the twentieth century and into the twenty-first, agitation in support of 'education for change' supplanted the established tradition of 'education for security' so far as British education policy was concerned. Certainly by the 1970s, and arguably before, reform of the education system had become a dominant concern of policy-makers promoting radical change.

Nevertheless, underlying the edifice of security, some key dynamics of insecurity were already present and active well before the Second World War. The first of these might be characterised as social anxiety. Joanna Bourke's study *Fear: A cultural history* explored the social and cultural dimensions of anxiety and fear, both private and public. It was a set of tensions to which the middle classes in particular were prey. As Bourke suggests, increased state provision of welfare diluted fear of poverty in the early twentieth century, but fears about social status grew: 'Rather than trembling about the effects of absolute privation, people shuddered to think about the consequences of *relative* impoverishment, such as being rehoused in a rougher area or forced to sell a prized possession' (Bourke 2005: 27). More generally, Peter Gay's history of the bourgeois experience of the nineteenth century – in his terms 'a family of desires and anxieties' – evokes a prevailing mood that was 'a mixture of helplessness and confidence', in which 'endemic excitement was controlled by social devices and private defences' (Gay 1984: 17, 67). The fears and anxieties of the middle classes constituted a destabilising influence long before the Second World War, hidden by the complacency of their characteristic rhetoric.

Ironically, it is the life and educational career of Cyril Norwood that is especially revealing in terms of middle-class social anxiety. Norwood himself came from a clerical, provincial middle-class background that was especially insecure due to his father, the Reverend Samuel Norwood, losing his post as headmaster of a grammar school and falling into an unhappy personal decline (see McCulloch 2006). He sought to alleviate the tensions that existed between the elite public schools and the new secondary education supported by the State. Yet, despite his success in being appointed first as master of Marlborough College and then as head of Harrow School, Norwood was never fully accepted by the elite groups that promoted and patronised the public schools. The foremost proponent of the 'English tradition of education' was also a victim of the acute awareness of social gradations that characterised the English middle classes.

Belying the outward appearance of stability and security, therefore, was an experience of insecurity that affected individuals and groups as a result of English preoccupations with social status and class. A further source of insecurity from the late nineteenth century onwards was an uncomfortable awareness of technical inferiority in relation to emerging rivals such as the United States and Germany. Periodic attempts to respond to such threats attest to the underlying anxieties that afflicted the body politic in this regard. These led, for example, to vocational reforms, especially in the 1890s and the 1920s, although such initiatives rarely lasted long and were limited in their effects (see e.g. McCulloch 1989; Sanderson 1994). By the 1950s, the prominent intellectual C.P. Snow drew attention to the loss of Britain's world position, which he attributed to the technological advances of the United States and the Soviet Union (Snow 1959). This general view helped to stimulate a further cycle of curriculum innovation in the

1960s. It also underlay debate around the causes of national decline, especially in the context of industrial and economic difficulties in the 1970s and 1980s (e.g. Roderick and Stephens 1979). Such tensions related directly to issues of national security, albeit that they centred on the implications of culture and technological change rather than on physical or military threats.

Insecurity and education policy debate

Taking such concerns into account, it might well be said that issues of security have shaped educational policy debates since the Second World War as much as those of change. Such debates have responded to a growing awareness of insecurity in a number of arenas, inducing an increasingly frenetic and unstable policy regime. The State has been drawn into matters of education policy on an ongoing and everyday basis, especially since the introduction of the Conservative reforms of the 1980s. These included the establishment of a National Curriculum, which meant state control of curriculum, pedagogy and assessment and stricter inspection. They also encouraged specialisation, diversity and parental choice, acknowledging anxieties over standards as well as continuing preoccupations about social differentiation.

The educational reforms of New Labour after 1997 if anything accelerated the pace of change. There was an atmosphere of policy neurosis, of policies announced, contradicted and discarded with unprecedented speed, of reforms 'gone before you know it' as in the case of the Education Action Zones (Franklin 2005). Like the Conservative reforms, too, they reflected a concern to limit the freedom that had previously been allowed to teachers and other educational professionals. In the case of schools this constrained teachers especially in the curriculum domain (see McCulloch 2001). In higher education, research, for example, came increasingly under the purview of the State (McCulloch 2003).

Within this overall context of frenetic policy change and the anxiety and insecurity which helped to maintain it, by the end of the twentieth century a new factor had developed to make national security a key issue. This was the emergence of a growing awareness of insecurity on a global scale. In part, this arose from a set of broad global issues that had a bearing on societies around the world. The global environment, for example, became a major concern as the nature and effects of 'global warming' became increasingly evident. The threat posed by the pandemic of AIDS and fears arising from such phenomena as 'bird flu' also raised awareness of health as a global issue. The changes in technology evident in the global spread of the Internet gave rise to a further set of issues that transcended national boundaries. Such developments posed a challenge to educational institutions to promote an informed awareness about risks and dangers among the population at large. At an ideological level, also, education was at the heart of a fresh debate about countering the novel influences impinging on Britain from elsewhere in these rapidly changing circumstances.

A prime example of this kind of development was the concern over defining and promoting 'Britishness' led by David Blunkett as Home Secretary. This represented a policy priority to use education as a device to inculcate patriotic values, and again was certainly not new in itself. During the Second World War, for instance, the prime minister, Winston Churchill, asked the new president of the Board of Education, R.A. Butler, to 'introduce a note of patriotism into the schools', on the grounds that, as he put it, 'Everyone has to learn to defend himself'. Butler demurred, pointing out that he 'would like to influence what was taught in schools but that this was always frowned upon', to which Churchill 'looked very earnest and commented, "Of course not by instruction or order but by suggestion"' (Butler 1973: 91). In the 1950s and 1960s, in the spirit of this exchange, the Ministry of Education generally resisted the temptation to enforce this kind of approach, but the introduction of the National Curriculum from 1988 engendered a new opportunity to do so.

The destruction of the Twin Towers in New York in September 2001, followed by the international 'war on terror' and conflict in Afghanistan and Iraq, created the motivation to make use of this opportunity. 'National security' now had both an ideological and a physical dimension, as Blunkett made plain. He was to the fore in promoting patriotism in schools and a more stringent process of acquiring British citizenship. An emphasis on the nature of British identity was part of this development. One commentator noted that this increasing attention to national identity was a 'defensive' project based on 'insecurity', 'driven at the macro level by an intensely competitive globalisation that has put most of the country's economic life beyond the power of the nation state, and at a micro level by individual economic welfare built on debt and a precarious jobs lottery'. The underlying basis for such debate, in this view, was a 'deep sense of insecurity' (Bunting 2005) that had long historical and cultural roots.

The shock induced by the bombings in London on 7 July 2005 served as the catalyst for further debate and stronger public measures. It was all too easy to contrast the role of Mohammed Sidique Khan as a learning mentor for children of immigrant families who had just arrived in Britain, with his supposed schooling of his fellow bombers on how to trigger their rucksack bombs at the same time (*The Times*, 14 July 2005: 1). The 'new wave of British terrorists', it was said, 'are taught at school, not in the mountains', and attention turned to a 'network of madrassas, the hardline religious schools, which have been blamed for turning out a generation of young jihadis' (*The Times*, 14 July: 8). Such accounts located schools as the focus of an ideological contest for 'hearts and minds'. In the universities also, there was a backlash against extremist behaviour, as the Secretary of State for Education, Ruth Kelly, demanded that universities inform the police about any concerns they had about 'unacceptable behaviour' or criminal acts (*The Times Higher Education Supplement*, 16 September 2005: 2). Security at campuses soon increased greatly as security budgets were increased by more than one-fifth, especially in London (ibid., 11 November 2005: 6). The emphasis here seemed to be on physical security, although concerns were also expressed about student societies that might be 'subversive' in character (Glees 2005).

Gordon Brown, Chancellor of the Exchequer, at the Royal United Services Institute in February 2006, raised all of these issues in a major speech. Under the title of 'Securing our future', this speech addressed the problems of national security, and pointed out the inextricable links between decisions in transport, energy, immigration, social security and health in countering external threats. It also recognised the significance of the changing character of technology, and the role of 'newspapers, journals, culture, the arts, literature' in enabling debate and dialogue over ideas. Moreover, Brown highlighted the ways in which personal identity was at risk with identities being 'stolen for terrorist or other reasons and used against us'. A national scheme of identity cards was proposed as an effective response to such dangers.

Lastly, Brown stressed the importance of education in promoting the ideals of Britishness in schools. This would include recognition of the contribution of the police, emergency and security services and of the armed forces in the great wars of the past century: 'Far from failing to teach history on these great times of conflict and courage we must do more to remember so that they will never be forgotten.' Further funding would be provided, Brown promised to support local ceremonies to celebrate ex-servicemen and women, and to promote an expansion of cadet forces in state schools. Indeed, Brown concluded,

> we should ask young people to play a leading role in future Veterans' Day celebrations – in particular volunteering to tape and video the memories of veterans for a veterans archive – led by a prominent national figure and supported by government and hopefully lottery funding – so that we have a local and national record of pride and achievement that measures up to the contribution our armed forces have made.
>
> (Brown 2006)

There was more than a little in this of Churchill's request to Butler during the Second World War to 'introduce a note of patriotism in our schools', with much more enthusiasm to carry it out. At the same time, a *Guardian* newspaper leader was quick to note a strong echo of American attitudes:

> It seemed to owe much – too much – to American thinking and models, with its calls for a new cultural cold war, its emphasis on a conflict that could last for generations, its talk of a global battle for hearts and minds, and its suggestions of a new department of national security and even for a new national veterans' day – the very term is an American import.
>
> (*Guardian*, 14 February 2006: 34)

In this link with the approach adopted by the American administration under George W. Bush, the deeply rooted security concerns of the United States, recurring at different stages over the past century, appear to have at last found clear resonance in the British response to their own insecurities.

Conclusion

These general reflections on the history of education and national security suggest that there is a rich research agenda to be developed further in this area. First, it seems important to examine in greater detail the historical significance of insecurity in British educational history. Insecurity of different types was already well established by the time that Clarke wrote his influential book at the start of the Second World War, and it has become increasingly pervasive over the decades since then. In the process, adopting the terms proposed by Karl Mannheim, it has generated a preoccupation with 'education for security' at the same time that there has developed a culture of 'education for change'. This looks increasingly like a structural or cultural shift, as opposed to a temporary adaptation to particular short-term events, that is medium and long term in its origins, characteristics and consequences.

This theme also raises the issue of differences and similarities in relation to the experiences of other nations over the past 50 years.

'National security' has played itself out in a distinctive way in the British context as opposed to that of the United States, for example. Yet there are also clear suggestions of transatlantic influence in this area, in which security issues become increasingly prominent, perhaps still mediated by social class but with a fundamentally changed outlook on global relationships. It will be necessary to search for evidence of such connections and influences, and on their characteristic effects. We may even need to look more closely at the institutions and curricula of the past 50 years to discover the extent to which security issues have influenced these. In the light of a changing present in which national security has come to the fore, we must bring ourselves to re-examine the lessons of our past.

References

Aldrich, R. (1997) *The End of History and the Beginning of Education*. London: Institute of Education.

— (2006) *Lessons from History of Education: The selected works of Richard Aldrich*. London: Routledge.

Barnett, C. (1986) *The Audit of War: The illusion and reality of Britain as a great nation*. London: Macmillan.

— (1995) *The Lost Victory: British dreams, British realities, 1945–1950*. Basingstoke: Macmillan.

Board of Education (1943) *Curriculum and Examinations in Secondary Schools* (Norwood Report). London: HMSO.

Bourke, J. (2005) *Fear: A cultural history*. London: Virago.

Brown, G. (2006) 'Securing our future'. Speech delivered at the Royal United Services Institute, London, 13 February. London: HM Treasury.

Bunting, M. (2005) 'Beyond Englishness'. *Guardian*, 14 March.

Butler, R.A. (1973) *The Art of the Possible*. London: Penguin.

Chomsky, N., Nader, L., Wallerstein, I., Lewontin, R.C., Ohmann, R., Zinn, H. et al. (1997) *The Cold War and the University: Toward an intellectual history of the postwar years*. New York: New Press.

Clarke, F. (1940) *Education and Social Change: An English interpretation*. London: Sheldon Books.

Foster, S. (2000) *Red Alert! Educators confront the red scare in American public schools, 1947–1954*. New York: Peter Lang.

Foster, S. and Davis, O.L. Jr (2004) 'Conservative battles for public education within America's culture wars: poignant lessons for today from the red scare of the 1950s'. *London Review of Education*, 2(2), 123–35.

Franklin, B. (2005) 'Gone before you know it: urban school reform and the short life of the Education Action Zone initiative'. *London Review of Education*, 3(2), 3–27.

Gay, P. (1984) *The Bourgeois Experience, Victoria to Freud. Vol. I: Education of the Senses*. Oxford: Oxford University Press.

Glees, A. (2005) 'Beacons of truth or crucibles of terror?' *The Times Higher Education Supplement*, 23 September, 16.

Hobsbawm, E. and Ranger, T. (eds) (1983) *The Invention of Tradition*. Cambridge: Cambridge University Press.

Hofstadter, R. (1966) *The Paranoid Style in American Politics, and Other Essays*. London: Cape.

Lowe, R. (2005) *Whatever Happened to Progressivism? The demise of child-centred education in modern Britain*. London: Institute of Education.

McCulloch, G. (1989) *The Secondary Technical School: A usable past?* London: Falmer.

— (2001) 'The reinvention of teacher professionalism'. In R. Phillips and J. Furlong (eds) *Education, Reform and the State: Twenty-five years of politics, policy and practice*. London: RoutledgeFalmer.

— (2003) 'Towards a social history of educational research'. In J. Nixon, P. Sikes and W. Carr (eds) *The Moral Foundations of Educational Research: Knowledge, inquiry and values*. Maidenhead: Open University Press.

— (2006) 'Cyril Norwood and the English tradition of education'. *Oxford Review of Education*, 32(1), 55–69.

— (2007) *Cyril Norwood and the Ideal of Secondary Education*. New York: Palgrave Macmillan.

McCulloch, G. and Richardson, W. (2000) *Historical Research in Educational Settings*. Maidenhead: Open University Press.

Norwood, C. (1929) *The English Tradition of Education*. London: John Murray.

Roderick, G. and Stephens, M. (eds) (1979) *Where Did We Go Wrong? Industrial performance, education and the economy in Victorian Britain*. London: Falmer.

Rudolph, J. (2002) *Scientists in the Classroom: The Cold War reconstruction of American science education*. New York: Palgrave.

Samuel, R. (1999) *Island Stories: Unravelling Britain. Vol. II: Theatres of Memory*. London: Verso.

Sanderson, M. (1994) *The Missing Stratum: Technical school education in England, 1900–1990*. London: Athlone Press.

Snow, C.P. (1959) *The Two Cultures and the Scientific Revolution*. Cambridge: Cambridge University Press.

Wiener, M. (1981) *English Culture and the Decline of the Industrial Spirit, 1850–1980*. Cambridge: Cambridge University Press.

Richard Aldrich: publications 1973–2006

Books and monographs

Sir John Pakington and National Education, Leeds: University of Leeds, 1979.

An Introduction to the History of Education, Sevenoaks: Hodder and Stoughton, 1982 (Chinese edition, 1987).

Education: Time for a new act? London: Institute of Education, 1985 (with P. Leighton).

Dictionary of British Educationists, London: Woburn Press, 1989 (with P. Gordon).

Education and Policy in England in the Twentieth Century, London: Woburn Press, 1991 (with P. Gordon and D. Dean).

History in the National Curriculum, London: Kogan Page, 1991 (editor).

School and Society in Victorian Britain: Joseph Payne and the new world of education, New York: Garland, 1995 (paperback edition, Theydon Bois: College of Preceptors, 1995).

Education for the Nation, London: Cassell, 1996 (Japanese edition, 2001).

In History and in Education: Essays in honour of Peter Gordon, London: Woburn Press, 1996 (editor).

Education and Cultural Transmission, Gent: CSHP, 1996 (*Paedagogica Historica* Supplementary Series II, co-edited with J. Sturm, J. Dekker and F. Simon).

The End of History and the Beginning of Education, London: Institute of Education, 1997.

Biographical Dictionary of North American and European Educationists, London: Woburn Press, 1997 (with P. Gordon*).*

The National Curriculum beyond 2000: The QCA and the aims of education, London: Institute of Education, 1998 (with J. White).

Faiths and Education, Gent: CSHP, 1999 (*Paedagogica Historica* Supplementary Series V, co-edited with J. Coolahan and F. Simon).
Education and Employment: The DfEE and its place in history, London: Institute of Education, 2000 (with D. Crook and D. Watson).
History of Education for the Twenty-first Century, London: Institute of Education, 2000 (co-edited with D. Crook).
A Century of Education, London: RoutledgeFalmer, 2002 (editor).
The Institute of Education 1902–2002: A centenary history, London: Institute of Education, 2002.
Public or Private Education? Lessons from history, London: Woburn Press, 2004 (editor).
Lessons from History of Education: The selected works of Richard Aldrich, London: Routledge, 2006.

Chapters in books

'W.E. Hickson and the *Westminster Review*, 1840–51', in R. Lowe (ed.) *Biography and Education: Some eighteenth- and nineteenth-century studies*, Leicester: History of Education Society, 1980.
'New history: an historical perspective', in A.K. Dickinson, P.J. Lee and P.J. Rogers (eds) *Learning History*, London: Heinemann Educational Books, 1984.
'The National Curriculum: an historical perspective', in D. Lawton and C. Chitty (eds) *The National Curriculum*, London: Institute of Education, 1988.
'Imperialism in the study and teaching of history', in J.A. Mangan (ed.) *'Benefits Bestowed'? Education and British imperialism*, Manchester: Manchester University Press, 1988.
'The evolution of teacher education', in N. Graves (ed.) *Initial Teacher Education: Policies and progress*, London: Kogan Page, 1990.
'Elementary education, literacy and child employment in mid-nineteenth-century Bedfordshire: a statistical study', in G. Genovesi, B.B. Gundem, M. Heinemann, J. Herbst, T. Harbo and T. Sirevag (eds) *History of Elementary School Teaching and Curriculum*, Hildesheim: Lax, 1990.
'The historical dimension' (with D. Dean), in R. Aldrich (ed.) *History in the National Curriculum*, London: Kogan Page, 1991.
'History in the National Curriculum in England: an historical perspective', in A.K. Dickinson (ed.) *Perspectives on Change in History Education*, London: Institute of Education, 1992.

'Discipline, practice and policy: a personal view of history of education', in K. Salimova and E. Johanningmeier (eds) *Why Should We Teach History of Education?* Moscow: Rusanov, 1993.

'The emerging culture of educational administration: a UK perspective', in Australian Council for Educational Administration, *The Emerging Culture of Educational Administration*, Darwin: ACEA, 1993.

'Vocational education in Britain: an historical and cultural analysis', in A. Heikkinen (ed.) *Vocational Education and Culture – European Prospects from History and Life History*, Tampere: Tampereen Yliopisto, 1994.

'Educational reform and curriculum implementation in England: an historical interpretation', in D.S.G. Carter and M.H. O'Neill (eds) *International Perspectives on Educational Reform and Policy Implementation*, London: Falmer Press, 1995.

'Historical perspectives upon current educational policy in England', in A. Heikkinen (ed.) *Vocational Education and Culture – European Prospects from Theory and Practice*, Tampere: Tampereen Yliopisto, 1995.

'Education and cultural Identity in the United Kingdom' (with A. Green), in B. Hildebrand and S. Sting (eds) *Erziehung und Kulturelle Identität*, Münster: Waxmann, 1995.

'Joseph Payne: an international educationist', in C. Wulf (ed.) *Education in Europe: An intercultural task*, Münster: Waxmann, 1995.

'History in education', in J. Sturm, J. Dekker, R. Aldrich and F. Simon (eds) *Education and Cultural Transmission*, Gent: CSHP, 1996 (*Paedagogica Historica* Supplementary Series II).

'Apprenticeship in England: an historical perspective', in A. Heikkinen and R. Sultana (eds) *Vocational Education and Apprenticeships in Europe – Challenges for Practice and Research*, Tampere: Tampereen Yliopisto, 1997.

'Education as a university subject in England: an historical interpretation' (with D. Crook), in P. Drewek and C. Lüth (eds) *History of Educational Studies, Geschichte der Erziehungswissenschaft, Histoire des Sciences de l'Education*, Gent: CSHP, 1998 (*Paedagogica Historica* Supplementary Series III).

'The role of the individual in educational reform', in C. Majorek, E. Johanningmeier, F. Simon and W. Bruneau (eds) *Schooling in Changing Societies: Historical and comparative perspectives*, Gent: CSHP, 1998 (*Paedagogica Historica* Supplementary Series IV).

'Teacher training in London', in R. Floud and S. Glynn (eds) *London Higher: The establishment of higher education in London*, London: Athlone Press, 1998.

'Joseph Lancaster: an individual and institutional appreciation', in Núcleo de Análise e Intervenção Educacional (ed.) *Ensaios em homenagem a Joaquim Ferreira Gomes*, Coimbra: University of Coimbra, 1998.

'Education and employment in England: historical perspectives, research and teaching' (with D. Crook), in A. Heikkinen, T. Lien and L. Mjelde (eds) *Work of Hands and Work of Minds in Times of Change*, Jyväskylä: University of Jyväskylä, 1999.

'The apprentice in history', in P. Ainley and H. Rainbird (eds) *Apprenticeship: Towards a new paradigm of learning*, London: Kogan Page, 1999.

'Educational standards in historical perspective', in H. Goldstein and A. Heath (eds) *Educational Standards*, Oxford: Oxford University Press, 2000 (*Proceedings of the British Academy*, 102).

'Mathematics, arithmetic and numeracy: an historical perspective' (with D. Crook), in S. Bramall and J. White (eds) *Why Learn Maths?* London: Institute of Education, 2000.

'A contested and changing terrain: history of education in the twenty-first century', in D. Crook and R. Aldrich (eds) *History of Education for the Twenty-first Century*, London: Institute of Education, 2000.

'Education as nationbuilding: lessons from British history', in S. Vaage (ed.) *Education and Nationbuilding*, Volda: Volda University College, 2001.

'Family history and the history of the family', in R. Aldrich (ed.) *Public or Private Education? Lessons from history*, London: Woburn Press, 2004.

'Teacher training, teacher education and pedagogy', in D. Halpin and P. Walsh (eds) *Educational Commonplaces: Essays to honour Denis Lawton*, London: Institute of Education, 2005.

Journal articles

'Radicalism, national education and the grant of 1833', *Journal of Educational Administration and History*, 1973, 5(1), 1–6.

'H.H. Milman and popular education, 1846', *British Journal of Educational Studies*, 1973, 21(2), 172–9.

'Facts behind the figures, 1839–1859', *History of Education Society Bulletin*, 1974, 13, 25–9.

'Association of Ideas: the National Association for the Promotion of Social Science', *History of Education Society Bulletin*, 1975, 16, 16–21.

'Uncertain vintage: the origins of the Church of England Education Society', *History of Education Society Bulletin*, 1976, 18, 41–3.

Richard Aldrich: publications

'Literacy, illiteracy, semi-literacy and marriage registers', *History of Education Society Bulletin*, 1978, 22, 2–6.
'"The growing intelligence and education of the people"', *History of Education Society Bulletin*, 1978, 22, 48–50.
'Sir John Pakington and the Newcastle Commission', *History of Education*, 1979, 8(1), 21–31.
'"National education by rates or taxes . . ."', *Journal of Educational Administration and History*, 1980, 12(1), 25–30.
'Sir John Pakington and the Select Committee of 1865–66', *History of Education Society Bulletin*, 1980, 25, 45–50.
'Sir John Pakington and education in the West Midlands', *West Midlands Studies*, 1981, 14, 10–14.
'Peel, politics and education, 1839–1846', *Journal of Educational Administration and History*, 1981, 13(1), 11–21.
'1870: a local government perspective', *Journal of Educational Administration and History*, 1983, 15(1), 22–6.
'Educating our mistresses', *History of Education*, 1983, 12(2), 93–102.
'History of education in schools', *Teaching History*, 1984, 39, 8–10.
'Learning by playing', *Education Today*, 1985, 35(2), 28–36.
'History (of education) at the crossroads', *The Historian*, 1986, 11, 10–14.
'Sunday schools: a research report', *History of Education Society Bulletin*, 1986, 38, 14–17.
'Learning by faith', *Education Today*, 1986, 36(3), 4–14.
'Interesting and useful', *Teaching History*, 1987, 47, 11–14.
'Central issues in history of education: an English perspective', *Canadian History of Education Association Bulletin*, 1987, 4(3), 17–25.
'Student experiences of teaching practice, 1985–6: a study in professional education' (with P. Leighton), *Education Today*, 1988, 38(1), 53–65.
'Renewed school history: an Hungarian perspective', *Teaching History*, 1988, 52, 28–9.
'A common countenance: national curriculum and national testing in England and Wales', *Policy Explorations*, 1989, 4(1), 1–12. (Published by the University of British Columbia, Canada.)
'Class and gender in the study and teaching of history in England in the twentieth century', *Historical Studies in Education/Revue d'Histoire de l'Education*, 1989, 1(1), 119–35.
'School inspection: a research report', *History of Education Society Bulletin*, 1989, 43, 10–12.
'History of education in initial teacher education in England and Wales', *History of Education Society Bulletin*, 1990, 45, 47–53.

201

'The National Curriculum: an historical analysis', *Education Today*, 1990, 40(3), 13–17.

'History Working Group: Final Report 1990', *History of Education Society Bulletin*, 1990, 46, 12–15.

'Mechanics institutes in South-Eastern England: a research report', *History of Education Society Bulletin*, 1991, 48, 11–14.

'Always historicise? A reply to Keith Jenkins and Peter Brickley', *Teaching History*, 1991, 65, 8–12.

'Questões de gênero na história da educação na Inglaterra', *Educação em Revista*, 1991, 13, 47–54. (Published by the Federal University of Minas Gerais, Brazil.)

'ERASMUS', *Cambridge*, 1992, 29, 83–8.

'Educational legislation of the 1980s in England: an historical analysis', *History of Education*, 1992, 21(1), 57–69.

'Joseph Payne and the Denmark Hill Grammar School', *Camberwell Quarterly*, 1992, 94, 8–11.

'Joseph Payne and the Mansion Grammar School, 1845–63', *Leatherhead and District Local History Society Proceedings*, 1992, 5(5), 133–7.

'Education in Britain: what went wrong?' *Parliamentary Brief*, 1993, 2(7), 58–60.

'The real Simon Pure: Brian Simon's four-volume history of education in England', *History of Education Quarterly*, 1994, 34(1), 73–80.

'Pioneers of female education in Victorian Britain: a research report', *History of Education Society Bulletin*, 1994, 54, 56–61.

'Can schools teach teachers?', *Parliamentary Brief*, 1994, 3(3), 107–8.

'John Locke', *Prospects*, 1995, 24(1–2), 61–76.

'National and international in the history of education', *History of Education Society Bulletin*, 1995, 55, 7–10.

'Joseph Payne: the College of Preceptors Joseph Payne Memorial Lecture', *Education Today*, 1996, 36(3), 3–7.

'Teachers in England: their education, training and profession', *Bulletin of the UK–Japan Education Forum*, 1997, 5–22.

'Past and present, private and public in the history of education', *Bulletin of the UK–Japan Education Forum*, 1997, 47–63.

'From Board of Education to Department for Education and Employment', *Journal of Educational Administration and History*, 2000, 32(1), 8–22.

'Reflections on the recent innovation of the National Curriculum in England', *Chung Cheng Educational Studies*, 2002, 1(1), 65–89.

'The three duties of the historian of education', *History of Education*, 2003, 32(2), 133–43.

'The training of teachers and educational studies: the London Day Training College, 1902–1932', *Paedagogica Historica*, 2004, 40(5–6), 617–31.

'Research centres in the history of education: the MA in history of education at the Institute of Education, University of London, 1980–2005', *History of Education Researcher*, 2005, 75, 52–4.

'The Institute of Historical Research', *History of Education Researcher*, 2006, 77, 11–14.

Index